To Jenna
From Granny and Horn

Flight from Latvia

A Six-Year Chronicle

Christmas
2017

Dagnija Neimane

49 Oakland Terrace
Burlington, Vermont
05408

Cover photograph:
Bundesarchiv, Bild 183-R64866
Flüchtende Zivilbevölkerung mit Pferdegespannen in einem Waldstück, Oktober 1944, Autor: Budulis

ISBN-13: 978-0-9975533-0-7

DEDICATION

To the memory of my parents,

Alfrēds and Lidija Neimanis –

– with affection and gratitude.

Contents

	Acknowledgments	i
	Map of Latvia	ii
	Map of Europe	iii

Chapters

1	Džūkste	1
2	Flight across Latvia	28
3	Anniņa's Flight	52
4	The Ferry M/S Peter Wessel	62
5	Tētiņ's Search for Us	68
6	Germany and German-Occupied Poland	75
7	Podsedice	83
8	The War's End	97
9	Mariánské Lázně	112
10	To the American Zone	115
11	Amberg	121
12	Lauingen	126
13	Hermanis	139
14	Haunstetten	161
15	Mamma and Papus	213
16	Hochfeld and Gronau	236
	Afterword	243

ACKNOWLEDGMENTS

For obvious reasons, this story is less about my own impressions than those of others with whom I have communicated. Because of my age at the start of our flight, my real memory of events only starts with our life in Lauingen, Germany. It has been awakened by the photographs of the most pictured places there, the beautiful arbor and the staircase with the Grecian urn. Among the adults, my aunt Anna Sveķis and my father were able to recount the most complete stories. My father kept a painstaking account of what happened to us on any date, and this, along with his collection of old documents, all came together to paint a clear picture of what our life was like during those six years. Among my cousins, Austars Šnore, who was already eight years old at the start of our flight, told his story with the most mature eyes. To him, to my sister, Maruta Hiegel, and to other friends and relatives who added their memories, I am very indebted. I have learned from all of them, as I have from accounts in periodicals of the time. Thank you also to my daughter Rachel Thornton for her advice and technical help, and to Oskar Cerbins, for his guidance throughout. To all of them I am extremely grateful.

Estonia
Russia
Pernau
Ainazi
Pskow
Valmiera
Ostrow
River Velikaya
Ventspils
River Gauja
Sigulda
More
Riga
Kuldiga
Viesalgas
Tukums
Kemeri
Kegums
Opochka
Klostere
Dzukste
Maslenki
Kazdanga
Saldus
Dobele
Jelgava
Aizpute
Naudite
Zingi
River Daugava
Kapsede
Ezere
Tervete
Bauska
Liepaja
River Venta
Lithuania
Daugavpils

Den-
mark
Sweden
Latvia
Liepaja
Lithu-
ania
Putlos
Neumunster
Gotenhafen
Danzig
East
Prussia
GB
Bremerhafen
Schneidemuhle
Munster/Westfalen
Berlin
Posen
Nether-
lands
Germany
Warsaw
Zedelghem
River
Rhine
River Elbe
Litzmanstadt
Belgium
Lovosice
Poland
Plauen
River
Main
Podsedice
Aussig
Dlaskovice
Mannheim
Marienbad
Pilsen
Prague
Stuttgart
Amberg
Czechoslovakia
France
Lauingen
Nuremberg
Kleinkotz
Haunstetten/Hochfeld
Munich
Austria
River
Danube
Switzerland
Hungary

CHAPTER ONE

DŽŪKSTE

Džūkste is a small Latvian town which lies 66 km. southwest of Rīga, the capital, and 40 km. northwest of Jelgava. Named for a river in its north, it means a bog or swamp. In 1935 during the young independent country's period of economic prosperity, Džūkste was a lively community with a consumer market, four Latvian and two Jewish stores, four hairdresser salons, a book store, two cobblers, two butcher shops, two tack stores, two lumber yards, two mechanics, three clothiers, two carpenters, four smithies, a steam powered mill, and a sawmill. There was also a marketplace with a meat inspection station and an artesian well having a depth of 37 meters. Among the town's buildings were a town hall, a grade school, an almshouse, a police station, a tavern, and a church. The Džūkste townsfolk already numbered 601, and 107 houses lay scattered along the town's dirt roads.

Postal services in Latvia had already been established the year following the country's 1918 independence. The Džūkste post at that time was headquartered in the communal building, and it served not only the town but also much of the surrounding area. Later, as the town gradually increased in size, the Ministry of Communication came to realize the need for a separate post office building in Džūkste. To that end, it purchased a building through the Ministry of Welfare. This was the former *Baznīcas Krogs,* the Church Tavern, so called because it was near the town's church. To the left of the church tavern was a stable, as was often the case near taverns and churches for the clients and parishioners to use when they came by horse and carriage.

As the twentieth anniversary of Latvia's independence was soon approaching, efforts were underway to improve as many of its establishments as possible, and this took on a special effort in Džūkste. In two more years and at a cost of 10,000 Lats, the previously unsuitable tavern was rebuilt into an attractive and comfortable new post office.

The left half of the building became an apartment for the postmaster. The other half, consisting of a public room, the telephone center, and the postmaster's office, which was not more than a desk and a cabinet of cubby-holes into which mail was sorted, was devoted to the business matters of the nation's Post and Telegraph Services. A door led to a hallway from which another door led to the postmaster's family's apartment.

Now the only thing left is the apartment and the central post office. The building also serves as a small convenience store. A tall round metal stove in one corner heats the room, as I suppose it did in those days long ago. The stable has long been gone. The town's many specialty shops are also gone, as they are not needed. Džūkste lost very many of its residents during the tragic events of 1941 and 1944. Only recently has a mini supermarket sprung up in the town square. For other necessities, the inhabitants now drive to Dobele, to Jelgava, and even to Rīga.

Mārtiņš Vasips, the man who had been Džūkste's Postmaster for six years during the 1930s died in August 1939, and the postal service began the search for a new man to take his place. My father answered the call.

MY PARENTS MET IN EZERE, a town near the Lithuanian border, where my mother, Lidija Bištēviņš, worked as a clerk in the post office of which my father, Alfrēds Neimanis, was Postmaster. Lidija, pretty and shy, never liked to be photographed and often maneuvered to the background whenever a group picture was to be taken. In her youth she had dreamed of being a gymnast in the Olympics and worked hard to attain her goal, though without success. After graduating from the classical state high school in Jelgava, she subsequently went to work as a postal employee.

Alfrēds Neimanis was the second of four children born into a family in Valmiera. After serving the obligatory 18 months' service in the Signal Corps of the Latvian military, Alfrēds trained for work in the National Postal Service, just as his own father had done. As the Neimanis family could only finance the higher education of one of their children, all hopes were placed on the shoulders of the youngest, Edīte, who wished to become a doctor. Edīte enrolled in classes at the Rīga University for that purpose, and her three siblings generously contributed the money necessary to pay for her education.

Alfrēds and Lidija married in Rīga on Saturday, June 15, 1940, when he was 33 and she was 27. Lidija's sister, Anna Bištēviņš, and Alfrēds' sister, Edīte, were witnesses to the event. My parents' wedding did not take place in the new Ģertrude Church on Brīvības street, as it normally would have transpired. Rather, the couple took their vows at the home of the minister, the Reverend Freidenfelds, on Elizabetes street. The wedding had been somewhat hurriedly arranged. My mother was very embarrassed regarding the date of her marriage, never talked about it, and would have preferred to keep it a secret. She was, it turns out, already expecting, and circumstances such as these were not publicly welcomed. Years later, looking through photographs in a box, I did come upon a neat little card which had once served as the wedding announcement along with the date of the event. This I saw only once, and then never again.

The day of my parents' wedding, June 15, 1940, was unfortunately also the day that the Soviets crossed the Russian-Latvian border at Masļenki. Under cover of night, they killed the border guards and the guards' family members in a prelude to their invasion of Latvia, which took place the very next day. Obviously, it was an inauspicious day to celebrate the beginning of the couple's life together.

At the time of their marriage, Alfrēds was still the Postmaster of the Ezere Post Office, but by June 31, 1940, he became the Postmaster of Džūkste for the Post and Telegraph Department of Latvia.

On October 22, Alfrēds, whom we called "Tētiņ," moved into the post office apartment and brought his wife, Lidija, and brand new daughter, Maruta, born September 17, 1940, into their new home. There my father busied himself with his Postmaster duties. My mother "Mimmīte" tended the vegetable and flower gardens, raised chickens, and also her two daughters – Maruta, and me, Dagnija, born May 28, 1942. These were the war years, but as much as we were able, we had a pleasant and happy life there. In subsequent years in their exile from Latvia, my parents often spoke longingly of Džūkste. Uncertain as it was, life had to go on.

AS POSTMASTER, TĒTIŅ DREW a salary of some 300 Lats per month. Other postal employees earned only 120, and the office clerk merely 80 Lats. These old Lat bills are now, of course, obsolete, but some years ago I received two of the bills from a cousin who had purchased them in a flea market. These I showed to Tētiņ, who rubbed them between thumb and forefinger, as if trying to remember the feel of the old notes, recalling the time they were used as legal tender some 50 years previously.

"They were once worth a lot of money," he mused. "In those days a kilogram of butter cost one Lat, depending on what the dairies decided they needed to ask. Latvian butter in those days was considered the best in Europe."

Tētiņ had charge of several postal employees. One clerk sold stamps and distributed letters to the villagers, while another sorted mail. Three telephone operators, Mrs. Rutkis, Mrs. Bolande, and Mrs. Keidāns, whose husband was employed in Jelgava, worked the switchboard phones. The

Keidāns couple lived not far from the post office, in a house just beyond one of the Jewish shops.

According to a 1940 telephone book, in all of Džūkste, there were only about ninety telephones that year. The phone number of the post office was 32, and the number to our apartment, which also had a telephone, was 61. Incoming telegrams were, for the most part, read over the phone by the operators. Tētiņ himself was fluent in Morse code and would operate the system himself if necessary. He also had an assistant, an office worker named Klints. Two technical staffers whose job it was to repair the telephones, and a housekeeper, an older woman named Lībiņa completed the list of employees. Tētiņ insisted that the post office be spotless and that the floors are washed daily. "And they were," Mimmīte later assured us.

The poet Rita Gāle was born and raised in Džūkste. She was the daughter of the town's veterinary doctor, Andrējs Gāle, and attended school in Jelgava. In 1942, Rita was 17 years old and had just published her first poem. She often stopped at the post office on her way home from school, dressed in her school cap and uniform to get the family's mail. In the 1990s I sometimes met Rita Gāle when I attended a Latvian heritage camp in the Catskills. There I purchased one of her books of poetry, which she inscribed for my father, "a fellow *Džūkstenieks*."

After she and I talked about her latest visit to Džūkste from the U.S., she sent Tētiņ a copy of a video she had filmed there. A service commemorating the Christmas battles of 1944 is shown taking place in the ruins of the old church, the congregation standing in the cold and snow within the crumbled remaining outer church walls. Watching the film, a fleeting glance of the post office building was visible as the camera panned through the landscape. Tētin watched this video, eagerly leaning forward, looking for anything recognizable. I think that until seeing this film, he had not known about the destruction of the more than 255 year old Džūkste church, as he never mentioned it in his stories.

While writing this memoir, I tried to find out the exact date that the demolition had occurred, which in history books is noted as 1944, the same as our flight from Latvia. However when I posed this question to a historian in Džūkste, Edīte Baldere-Sildedze, she told me the following: "In 1944 Džūkste was not yet a front in the war. The church was still standing during the 1944 German-Soviet Christmas battles of the Courland Cauldron," and here her voice rose to impress upon me her irrefutable information. "It was not until February 1945, when the Soviets forced the German army to withdraw from the Džūkste area that the Germans demolished the church on the 16th of that month, leaving only the remnants of three of the outer walls. Its steeple, the highest point in the vicinity, would have been too convenient a vantage point for the advancing Russians."

MY ANCESTORS WERE SERFS who worked the land belonging to the Baltic German barons in Latvia. The abolishment of serfdom occurred in 1817, and a law in 1849 granted the creation of peasant-owned farms. The peasants, the former serfs, were allowed to purchase the barons' land upon which they had slaved for generations. My mother's grandfather, Jānis Bištēviņš, was thus able to buy the Bākuļi homestead located in Šķibe *pagasts* (district) near Dobele, where he lived. To earn enough money, Jānis worked in Jelgava as a teamster and after work walked or hitched a ride home, some 21 km. away. There he did the work which still needed to be done. At the end of the day, he often just sat down at the table and fell asleep, resting his head on his hand. In the morning it was again time to make his way to Jelgava and his teamster job. Years later he had earned enough money and was able to purchase Bākuļi.

With such transfers of land and property, a new class of independent farmers was established, and in the last part of the 19th century, the social structure and national identity of Latvians became very evident. This was not to the liking of Czar Alexander III of Russia, who instituted a Russification policy starting in the 1880s in an attempt to reduce the autonomy of the Baltics. In Latvia, Russian replaced the German and Latvian languages as the official language. This led to discontent, and along with other political and social unrest within the Russian Empire, the 1905 Revolution followed. It took on an especially nationalistic character in the Baltics, leading to armed conflict between the land-owning Baltic German nobility and the Latvian peasants. When the Czarist police intervened, they exiled thousands of Latvians to Siberia, the first of such deportations.

On August 1, 1914, at the beginning of the "Great War," Germany commenced warfare with Russia, and by 1915 the conflict had reached Latvia. On June 29 the Russian Supreme Command ordered the retreat of the population of Kurzeme (Courland, the western part of Latvia), and thousands of refugees fled eastward. Some settled in eastern Latvia but most continued on their way into Russia. This war also uprooted my father's Neimanis family members from the

Valmiera area and my mother's Bištēviņš family, who at the time lived in Pärnu in Estonia. It forced both families to seek sanctuary far from their homeland. Both families settled in the Ukraine and nearby areas of Russia during the war years, both of my parents being just young children.

MIMMĪTE'S MOTHER, "MAMMA," Marta Raudseps, was born in Ainaži in Latvia in 1887, one of eight children in the Raudseps family. Marta's father, Nikolajs Raudseps, was in his late 20s when he accompanied the Swedish sailor and explorer Christian Dahl on two expeditions to the Ob River Estuary in Siberia during 1876 and 1877. These expeditions established an Arctic route for commerce to the Ob River. Later Christian Dahl became the first director of the Ainaži Naval School, and when he transferred to the school in Liepāja, Nikolajs Raudseps took over his duties in Ainaži and served in that capacity from 1893 until the war in 1915. Because of the close ties between Ainaži and Pärnu in Estonia, students from the Ainaži Naval School took their examinations with the board in Pärnu, 68 km. to the north. Eventually several of the Raudseps children, including Marta, went to live and study in that city.

Mimmīte's father, "Papus," Eduards Bištēviņš, born in 1870, was the youngest son of Jānis Bištēviņš of the Bākuļi homestead. Eduards yearned for an education and set off to Moscow to study. After completion, he worked as a professor of classical languages in the Pärnu *Ģimnasium* (secondary school) in Estonia from 1900 to 1915. Papus was multilingual and fluent in eight languages. One of his students had been the Latvian Ambassador Edgars Krieviņš, who remarked about his professor, "I remember Bištēviņš as being an idealist pure in heart, more in touch with his ancient Greek and Roman world than with this present sorrowful province."

It was in Pärnu that Eduards made Marta's acquaintance. She was seventeen years his junior and also his student. They married in 1907 in the St. Nikolai church. The couple's first child, Kārlis, was born in 1909 but died at the age of three of diphtheria. Margarita "Rita" was born in 1910, and three more children – Hermanis in 1911, my mother Lidija in 1913, and Anna in 1916 – followed soon thereafter.

The Great War changed life in Estonia considerably. Money lost its value, the black market thrived, and factory closings led to unemployment. In early 1917, during the war's mass evacuation, Eduards Bištēviņš took his family and left Pärnu. They made their way to Yeysk, a town in Krasnodar Krai, Russia, on the shore of the Sea of Azov. There in 1920, another baby was born, but died that same year at the age of eight months. In 1921 the Bištēviņš family returned to an independent Latvia and took up residence in the city of Jelgava.

In August of that year, Eduards Bištēviņš was employed as a Latin teacher in the school which later became known as the *Hercog Pēter Ģimnazija.* During his later years, Papus' sight started to fail. This progressed slowly at first, but soon he recognized his students only by their voices, as by then his blindness was almost complete. Still, he continued to work, since working earned him more than a pension would have provided. Mamma helped with the preparation of his lessons. Even then his blindness did not inhibit his teaching. He knew every word of text by heart, and often could tell his students from which page in their textbooks he quoted. Papus didn't sit to deliver his lessons, but rather paced slowly at the head of his class. Blind and reserved as he was, the students could easily have taken advantage of him, but he was widely admired, and everyone treated him with respect. As the blindness progressed, he was tormented by flashes of light due to a malfunctioning of his optic nerves. Even an operation by a well-known specialist could not help, and finally he succumbed to complete darkness. Papus retired from his teaching profession at the close of the school year in 1936.

A word of explanation: we called our grandparents by the same names that their own children did. Thus Mimmīte's parents were known to us as Mamma and Papus. Tētiņ's parents were then Mammucītis and Pappucītis. This made things very easy for us and it lovingly identified our grandparents in our own little family circle. I shall continue to call them by these same names in this story. The tradition continues with my daughter Rachel, who refers to her grandparents by these same names.

MY FATHER'S FAMILY, THE NEIMANIS, originated from the area of Valmiera, in Vidzeme, the north-eastern part of Latvia. Alfrēd's father, Pēteris, had been a mailman, and also played the coronet in the Czar's army band. Pēteris married Marija Tančers in 1905. Marta Neimanis, the first daughter, was born in 1906, my father Alfreds in 1907, Andrejs in 1910, and Edīte in 1912.

During the Great War, all of the Czar's departments from that area had been moved out of Latvia to Russia or to the Ukraine. Pēteris' brother-in-law Kārlis Tančers, a staunch

Communist, had moved to the town of Bakhmach in the Ukraine, so it was also to Bakhmach that the Neimanis family emigrated. Tētiņ said that shortly after their arrival, in March of 1918, the Germans invaded the town. The following January, Bakhmach was in turn overtaken by the Bolsheviks. Because Tētiņ attended school there, he learned the Russian language before the family's return to Valmiera in 1921.

IT WAS DURING THESE FEW years in the absence of our parents' family members that Latvia declared sovereignty and became an independent country for the first time in 700 years, during which it had lived under German, Swedish, and Russian rule.

The Great War had ended on November 11, 1918, with the signing of the Armistice Treaty. It was also at that time that a breakdown of the Russian Empire occurred. Latvia declared itself to be an independent state on November 18 that same year. Great Britain announced its *de facto* recognition of Latvia on that day as well. During the years following the independence declaration, Latvia rebuilt its political, social, and economic life from the chaos left after the Great War. On September 22, 1921, it was admitted to membership in the League of Nations.

The years of this short period of independence were marked by an increase in nationalistic pride, productivity, and self-determination. During this time Latvia reached economic security and attained international respect. Especially in the latter 1930s, its growth resulted in a standard of living considered to be one of the highest in Europe. The first hydroelectric station at Ķegumi on the River Daugava was constructed with Swedish financial help, enabling ready and economical electric energy. Latvia became one of the leading exporters of butter, flax, timber, and other goods to countries across Europe. Even during times of economic depression on the continent, Latvia learned that it could sustain itself with its own grocery production.

WORLD WAR II HAD ALREADY started at the beginning of September in 1939. Though several countries, among which were Estonia, Latvia, and Lithuania, initially declared their neutrality, both the Soviets and Germany managed to dispute it that same month.

Germans had lorded over Latvian serfs for centuries. Now, because of outcomes of secret arrangements between Germany and Russia, and also because of treaties between the Baltic States of Latvia and Estonia, Nazi Germany urged the Baltic Germans to emigrate. In October of that year the first Latvian Germans left Latvia from Liepāja by ship to Gotenhafen for repatriation to Germany, where they settled in areas of Poland recently annexed by Nazi Germany. The returning Baltic Germans had to undergo lengthy physical exams with an emphasis on verification of their race. If they passed the examinations, they were given apartments or homes which the Poles had hurriedly abandoned to the Germans on their flight eastward.

Twenty-one short years after Latvia gained her independence, on August 23, 1939, Germany and the Soviet Union signed the Molotov-Ribbentrop Pact designed outwardly to ensure non-belligerence between the two nations. However, the pact included a secret protocol that put the Baltic countries and others under Soviet influence.

In October 1939, the Soviets demanded the establishment of military bases in Latvia in exchange for Stalin's false promise to respect Latvia's independence. Latvia could do nothing but submit to the ultimatum and accept the stationing of Soviet troops on her territory. The Soviets had already made provocative actions along the borders and in the air over the Baltic States. Now, after staging border incidents, they accused Latvia of breaching the agreement. On June 15, 1940, the day of Mimmīte and Tētiņ's wedding, they killed the guards at the Latvian-Russian border at Masļenki and forged their way inland. By the following day, they had invaded both Latvia and Estonia and by June 17, the Bolshevik invaders had also entered Lithuania. Both Latvia and Estonia realized that resistance would be hopeless and they capitulated.

The Latvian president Kārlis Ulmanis urged his people to comply without resistance to Soviet demands, and the overwhelmed Latvian government also relented. That day the Soviets occupied the communications facilities which included the post offices. In the coming days, the free press, the police, the defense organizations, and youth groups were all liquidated and forbidden to assemble. The most important public servants were either removed from duty or imprisoned. The jails quickly filled up, not with criminals and lawbreakers, but with Latvia's most devoted servants.

President Ulmanis was arrested and deported to Russia's interior. Newspapers reported that he had been executed. Latvia's Parliament met in a special session on August 4, at which an illegal "election" of new parliaments petitioned for incorporation as an equal member into the Union of Soviet States. This request was readily accepted. Thus Latvia, and likewise, Lithuania and Estonia became the 14th, 15th, and 16th Soviet republics.

Previously the Baltics had been somewhat on the sidelines observing Stalin and Hitler at odds with each other, but now they found themselves in Stalin's clutches with Germany's approval. The ensuing months would become known in Latvia as *Baigais Gads*, the Year of Horror.

To ensure absolute compliance, the Soviets set out to purge the country of anyone considered an enemy of the state. Thousands of people were arrested. The mass arrests, disappearances, deportations, tortures, and executions culminated on the night of June 14, 1941, the Day of Sorrow, with the deportation of 15,000 Latvians to Siberia. In that single night they were arrested, loaded onto trucks, and deposited at the train station named *Torņakalns* (Tower Hill) in Rīga where trains of cattle cars waited. Packed tightly into these, they were sent to prisons and labor camps in Siberia. The journey was long and without food and water. Many of them died along the way, and their bodies were simply thrown from the train. Arriving at their destination, without previous warning, the surviving men were separated from their families and sent farther inland to forced labor camps. During 1941, altogether some 34,000 people were enslaved, tortured, or killed. After years of their Siberian exile, if any were able to return to Latvia, they suffered forever from health ailments brought on by the harsh conditions they had endured.

Today at the *Torņakalns* railroad station, a single old cattle car wagon stands as a humble memorial. Just one kilometer away, the Victory Park monument, constructed during 1985 in Soviet Latvia, towers over the vicinity. This monument is a thorn in the side of all Latvians. Its eighty meter concrete obelisk and two groups of imposing statues symbolizing Mother Russia greeting her returning warriors commemorates Soviet Russia's "liberation" of Rīga from the German Reich.

ARRESTS FOR DEPORTATION were not only taking place in the cities, but even in small towns like our Džūkste. The minister, the regional secretary, and the postmaster, they all peered anxiously from their windows, watching the trucks laden with the unfortunates in the open wagons passing by. Anyone who had a profession considered more distinctive than that of farm laborers – teachers, ministers, town officials, and yes, even postmasters – was considered a potential threat to the Soviets. They could become an unnecessary problem and a hazard which needed to be zealously eliminated.

So the Džūkste residents watched, wondering if the trucks would stop at their own homes and arrest them for deportation to Siberia. However, the trucks disappeared down the road and once more the earlier stillness descended upon the town. The people gazing out of their windows seemed to again be able to breathe deeply, at least for the moment. Altogether forty-five of the inhabitants of the Džūkste district had been exiled to Siberia in 1941.

When the Soviets entered Džūkste they immediately took over the municipal offices and their workers. The community council secretary A. Mellupe, who had that role during at least the previous two years, continued to work in that capacity under the Soviets. Mimmīte had always been socially friendly with everyone and she had an amicable relationship with Mrs. Mellupe. After the trucks with their prisoners left Džūkste for their rendezvous with the cattle cars destined for Siberia, Mimmīte made a visit to A. Mellupe.

Stepping into her office, she dared to ask, "Is our family also on the list of people to be deported?"

It did not take long for Mrs. Mellupe to glance onto her sheet of pending departures, and she whispered to Mimmīte, "Yes, your family is on the list."

Mrs. Mellupe seemed to have knowledge of practically everything going on in Džūkste.

At the time, Marutiņa was only nine months old, and Mimmīte was not even yet pregnant with me. Now our parents knew what their fate would be. The first trucks had left Džūkste, but they would soon be back again. Who knew what awaited us and the others who had fearfully watched the departing trucks? What could we possibly do?

WHAT TURNED OUT TO BE barely a week after the June 14 Day of Sorrow, on June 22, 1941, Adolf Hitler put his planned attack of the Soviet Union, Operation Barbarossa, into effect. During the German invasion, four million Axis power soldiers invaded the USSR along a 2900 km. front, the most extensive invasion in history. The Germans quickly advanced through Lithuania toward Daugavpils in the south of Latvia. After the June atrocities by the Soviets toward the civilians, a period of quiet reprieve seemed to descend over the area. The Bolsheviks were forced to pull their troops out of Latvia since they needed to regroup their armies into a defense of their Russian homeland. The Nazi offensive seemed to have disrupted their plans to deport several hundred thousand more from the Baltic countries on June 27 and 28 in 1941.

Germany had never been historically considered Latvia's friend. However, after 1941 when it seemed to have interrupted further Soviet brutalities, the Latvians greeted them almost as liberators even though the Nazis did not reinstate Latvian sovereignty. At least the Germans were fighting the Russians, and as long as this situation stayed in effect there was hope that we would not be sent to Siberia. In relief the Latvian national anthem was once more being played on the radio.

What the Latvians couldn't predict was that once Nazi Germany set foot on Latvian soil, they would continue with their plans for the "final solution." The killings of Jews were systematically conducted wherever Nazi Germany occupied territory. Wasting no time, the first executions in Latvia already took place on the night of June 23 during the first days of Barbarossa. A paramilitary force, the Latvian Auxiliary Police, was created from Latvian volunteers by the Nazi German authorities. These units participated in the looting from and the killing of the local Jewish population.

Some 40 km from Džūkste, 2000 Jews were exterminated in Jelgava and its environs, and the main Jelgava synagogue was burned. Mass killings continued in Liepāja, which saw the murder of 700 Jews in early July. In Rīga, more synagogues were torched. One such brutality occurred on Stabu street, just one block from where my 2004 apartment was. There 30 Jews were dragged from their nearby homes and locked inside the synagogue, after which it was set on fire.

Yet the worst massacre in Latvia occurred during two days, November 30 and December 8 that same year. 25,000 Jews were killed in or on the way to Rumbula, a forest near Rīga. Some of these were German Jews transported by train from Germany expressly for the slaughter. Altogether 90% of Latvia's Jewish population was exterminated during the Holocaust. 90,000 people were killed by the Nazis in Latvia. Of these, 70,000 were Jews. The rest were principally civilians whose politics and activities were not acceptable to the German occupiers.

Even our town of Džūkste did not escape the horror. Just beyond the post office was a small store owned by a Jew where we had bought sugar, flour, and oatmeal, among other things, and where Tētiņ had always purchased petrol for our lamps. The storekeeper lived there with his wife and two-year-old daughter. One day in 1942 or 1943, when the stories of actions taken by the Germans incited them, or when the Latvian Auxiliary Police goaded them on, the Džūkste partisans invaded the store and looted it of everything. During this invasion the Jewish family disappeared, and Tētiņ feared that they had been murdered by the villagers. At any rate, nobody heard from them any more. The husband of the telephone operator, Mrs. Rutkene, a police officer, came by the post office and told Tētiņ that he should hurry and get whatever he wanted from the store before it was all gone. Even the thought of that was deplorable to Tētiņ. Later, when he went to look at the devastation, the store had been stripped completely bare.

DURING THIS OCCUPATION, our family could do nothing to protect our own possessions from the German invaders, who came and helped themselves to whatever they wanted. Latvian winters were unusually cold. Tētiņ had chopped wood which was to last all winter, but the Germans came and took all of it. They also killed and ate our chickens. They were the occupying force and they did whatever they pleased. The German occupation of Latvia lasted for another four years, until 1945 and the end of the war in Europe.

Tētiņ's father, Pappucītis, came to visit us in Džūkste in 1942. It was the last time that Tētiņ saw him, as when Pappucītis returned to Valmiera, we would remain in Džūkste only two more years.

Sometime during the German years Tētiņ's brother, Andrejs, who was a food store proprietor in Valmiera also came for a visit. I had come into the world in May of 1942, and it was probably on the occasion of my baptism, as he became my godfather. With him was his big hunting dog, Floka. Because Andrejs would not be returning directly to Valmiera, he temporarily left Floka with us in Džūkste. Floka seemed happy to be there, but at one point the dog slipped out of his leash and took off at a run. Tētiņ followed at a fast clip calling for Floka, but the faster Tētiņ ran, the more Floka enjoyed the race. Finally, it was Tētiņ who gave up and returned home, thinking that Floka would soon get tired of his little adventure and come back for his supper.

But Floka did not return. Some three hours later, a convoy of German military cars passed through Džūkste. Who should be sitting there in the passenger seat of the lead car but Floka, proudly looking straight ahead with not even a glance at poor Tētiņ. There was no use for Tētiņ to protest

Floka's act of revolt. He would have had to deal with the invading German force, and he was not up to that challenge. So he stood helplessly and watched Andrejs' beloved Floka disappear with his newly chosen comrades.

NEAR DOBELE IN THE AURI district and easily reachable from both Jelgava and Džūkste was the Ziņģi homestead. The farm was a reasonably large property surrounding a cluster of red brick buildings which included living quarters for servants. Ziņģi belonged to Alīse Silenieks, the niece of Mimmīte's father. Alīse Uice had married the landlord of Ziņģi, Karl Brederman, who after seven years of marriage died of tuberculosis. In 1924, Alīse married again. Her new husband Pēteris Silenieks was a *Pulkvedis* (Colonel) in the Latvian army. During the 1930s, the years of Latvia's prosperity, the couple traveled throughout Europe. At Ziņģi they had several maids and farm laborers helping with the work. Especially during the harvest and planting seasons, other farm help was brought in whenever more was needed. Pēteris Silenieks himself also worked in the fields, at times attired in his army uniform.

The Bištēviņš clan was quite sociable and there are many photographs of celebrations throughout the years, most often taking place at Ziņģi, which was large enough to accommodate everyone. One photograph shows the wedding of a Ziņģi maid, with Bištēviņš family members interspersed among those of the bride and groom's family. Alīse was a very hospitable woman and her door seemed to always be open. Summers for the Jelgava Bištēviņš were often spent at her farm, especially our summers, those of the five young cousins, the children of the Bištēviņš sisters.

My cousin Stariņ remembers the summer of 1942 in Ziņģi:

> There were about five Russian POWs helping with the harvest. They did not stay at the farm, but came when needed in a truck. I remember them as carefree, happy-go-lucky guys, nothing that you would expect of a POW. German soldiers also, who had not fully recovered from wounds were sent to Ziņģi, two or three at a time.

One of them, with a Lithuanian last name, taught Stariņ's mother, Rita, this verse:

Ach, lieber Gott, mach mich doch blind,
Dass ich den Goebbels arisch find.
Ach, lieber Gott, mach mich doch taub,
Dass ich an all das Unsinn glaub.
Ach, lieber Gott, mach mich doch stumm,
Dass ich nicht ins Dachau kumm.
Dann bin ich blind, taub, stumm zugleich,
Dann bin ich reif fuers dritte Reich.

(Oh, dear God, make me blind
So that Goebbels looks Aryan to me.
Oh, dear God, make me deaf,
So that I believe all of the absurdity.
On, dear God, make me mute,
So that I'm not sent to Dachau.
Then I'll be blind, deaf, and mute,
And ready for the Third Reich.)

There was another one:

Komm Adolf Hitler sei unser Gast,
und gib uns die Hälfte von dem was du hast;
aber nicht Pellkartoffeln und Hering,
sondern was du isst und Göring.

(Come Adolf Hitler and be our guest,
And give us half of what you have;
Though not boiled potatoes and herring,
But that what you eat, and also Göring.)

These were examples of the *Flüsterwitze*, so-called "whisper jokes" which in those days one did not repeat too loudly for obvious reasons.

Image from Džūkste by K Straubergs and J. Straubergs

Džūkste post office in 1938

Image source Zudusi Latvija

Džūkste, pre-1945

Džūkstes pagasta valde ar darbiniekiem.
I. rindā no kr. 1) pag. v. loc. Ed. Freimanis, 2) v. l. c. un pag vec. vietn. R. Niedra, 3) pag. vec. R. Kažotnieks, 4) pag. sekr. J. Baums, 5) v. loc. K. Šverins un 6) Ed. Steinerts, II. rindā no kr. 1) kanclejas ier. E. Pētersone un 2) V. Dicis, 3) sekr. pal. A. Mellupe, 4) kanclejas ierēd. V. Pēda, 5) rev. kom. priekšsēd. O. Gailis, 6) rev. kom. loc. R. Brakmanis un 7) P. Strauss.

Image from Džūkste by K Straubergs and J. Straubergs

The Džūkste district officials and staff in 1938.

2nd row, 3rd left: the secretary A. Mellupe.
1st row, 3rd left: Roberts Kažotnieks, the town elder.
2nd row, 5th left: Otto Gailis

Both Roberts Kažotnieks and Otto Gailis
were among those exiled to Siberia in 1941.

The Bištēviņš Family, 1927
Eduards and Marta with their children
Margarita, Anna, Lidija, and Hermanis

The Neimanis Family, 1935
Pēteris and Marija with their children
Alfrēds, Edīte, Marta, and Andrejs

Alfrēds in Blīdene, outside the train station post office.

Lidija Bištēviņš

CHAPTER TWO

FLIGHT ACROSS LATVIA

Bēglis

Ko paņēmu līdzi? Visdārgāko!
No mātes man asaru spožums.
No līgavas sāpju vaids –
Un rokā balts ceļa spieķis,
Un sirdī – izmisums, naids.

No mājām man pelnu sauja,
Zem kājām rudens dūksts ...
Andrejs Eglītis

The Refugee

What did I take with me? The most precious!
From mother the shine of her tears.
From my beloved, her grievous moan –
In hand a white walking stick,
In my heart – despair, hatred.

From home a handful of dust,
Under my feet the autumn slough …
Andrejs Eglītis

In late 1941 upon the U.S.'s entry into the war and its alliance with the British, it soon became obvious that the Allies could not attain a decisive victory over Nazi Germany without the aid of the Soviets on the Eastern Front. The Germans posed a much greater threat to world peace than Soviet Russia, and to defeat it President Roosevelt confided that he "would hold hands with the devil" if necessary. As for the Russians, the June 1941 Nazi Barbarossa invasion of the Soviet Union convinced Stalin that he could not do without the help of the U.S. and British armies. So it was that when the United States entered the war as a belligerent in December of 1941, it did so in partnership with the Soviets and the British as Allies.

In the spring of 1942, Hitler decided to mount further offensives with the aim of capturing the oil-rich Caucasus (where Anniņa's husband Juris Sveķis perished) and the city of Stalingrad. However, poor strategic management of the German troop locations brought the Nazis to a stalemate in Stalingrad and also to a turning point for the war in the East.

Finally, on D-Day, June 6, 1944, the U.S., British, and Canadian forces launched the invasion of France on the Normandy coast. This turn in the tide of war was what Stalin had been eagerly awaiting. By mid-July in 1944 the Soviet Army had once again crossed Latvia's pre-war eastern border. Battles were already being waged on Latvian territory, and the inhabitants of the southeastern part of Latvia, Latgale, were fleeing. The horrific events of June 1941 were fresh in their memories, and nobody wanted to experience the inevitable repetition. Some fled south by train to Germany or traveled over land by horse and wagon. If there was time, they quickly grabbed what they could of precious mementos and family photographs, as these were irreplaceable.

Those more perceptive realized that leaving Latvia was a permanent solution and that there would be no hope of returning, no matter how much one would wish. It was most certainly these same individuals who packed up a bit of Latvian earth, a final souvenir of the homeland which they would never see again. Years later when living in Milwaukee, I attended a funeral of one of these exiles and observed that a handful of this precious earth was the first that was scattered onto the coffin. Thus the refugee's final resting place was under Latvian soil, after all.

THE LATVIANS SOON DISCOVERED what being attacked by the Soviets really meant. Making their way across Latvia from the east, the Russians destroyed everything that they encountered. If not readily able at any given moment to commit their own atrocities, the Soviets depended on what became known as the "Bolshevik bandits." These "bandits" acted as spies and provided reconnaissance, thus weakening resistance in readiness for the Soviet invaders who soon followed. They were not a division of the regular Soviet army, but were comprised of remnants of destroyed companies, escaped Red Army prisoners, and criminals to whom the prison door had been left wide open: robbers and murderers who delighted in acts of sadistic brutality. Often they wore civilian garb or stolen German uniforms. In the dark of night they mined or unscrewed train tracks, and waylaid, robbed, or murdered travelers. They poisoned wells, burned children's sanctuaries, defiled churches, and otherwise terrorized the local inhabitants.

Wherever the Soviets conquered ground, they conscripted men between the ages of 18 and 50 into the Soviet army, and these conscripts were immediately sent to the front. One such company of eighty unfortunates was commanded to mount the attack of a railroad station. If the men fell from exhaustion they were shot from behind. Though their capture of the station succeeded, of eighty men only twenty-nine survived. The Soviet army continually resorted to using conscripts to lead offensives such as these. Altogether some 60,000 were drafted into the Red Army, and they often had to fight against other Latvians who had joined the legionnaires on the German side. At least half of these Latvians were killed in this war in which their country had never been the aggressor.

Arriving at a farmhouse, hamlet, or small town, the Soviets robbed its inhabitants of all they possessed. The residents were forced to emerge from their homes carrying all of their food stores. Anyone trying to hide any was shot. Men capable of carrying firearms were drafted into the Red Army. The rest, fifteen to sixty year olds, were forced into labor. Church ministers and teachers, considered to be enemies of the Soviet system, were segregated from other townspeople and were immediately shot. Altogether over two thirds of Latvia's intellectuals, academics, and other professionals – the scientists, writers, and town officials, hearing of the slaughter, chose to flee.

Many farmers hitched their horses or oxen to carriages and tried to make their way to the western harbors of Liepāja and Ventspils. As they embarked on any ship that would take them to Germany or Sweden, they had no other choice but to abandon their animals at the harbor.

On July 24, 1944, the Soviets already reached the city of Jelgava, and the bombing commenced in earnest soon thereafter. To ensure the destruction of rail connections with Rīga, Jelgava's railroad station became the primary target. This bombing also demolished four long trains filled with refugees waiting to depart. Within an hour the city was transformed into burning piles of debris. Still, small groups of the town's defenders fought on. However, on August 6, the Soviets attacked in force and after two more days of bloody combat, Jelgava was lost.

At the end of July in 1944, Gunars Birkmanis, a young boy at the time, described what he observed from his home in the village of Naudite, just 10 km. from Ziņģi:

> The fires from Jelgava could be seen burning for several days, the flames especially visible during the night from our town of Naudite 30 km. away. During the last three

days and nights of July, an unending stream of horse-drawn carriages driven by farmers in worn gray work clothes wove down the main road by day, fewer at night. Aged mournful women and weary children sat on sacks full of their belongings in the wagons. Other women and children could be seen herding their animals which now and again attempted to leave the road and foray into a field to snatch a mouthful of clover or some other delectable morsel. A few groups of young legionnaire boys from the Jelgava barracks joined the stream of refugees. They had run away when the barracks were invaded by the Soviet tanks. The boys, still dressed in the army's gray-green uniforms, had just recently been admitted to the Legion. They had not yet undergone training and were incapable of handling firearms…

The road ran partly through our family's fields, and in the evening, Father went down to the refugees to invite them to allow their animals to feed on the abundant clover. At night I could hear every small sound from the road and felt sorry for each refugee who had left his home and was now on the way to foreign places. I felt that Zemgale was forever losing all of these thousands of people and that the land would be left barren and empty. Mother and I were convinced that we too should gather what we could and join the flight. It was difficult to imagine that all of a sudden, we would have to abandon everything – the newly built home, the young apple trees bearing their first fruit, the lovingly cared for animals. Father contradicted us – our family had no history of any anti-Soviet deeds. "The war will end, and everyone shall come back," he explained.

However, everything happened otherwise. Staying close to home, we witnessed the devastation that the Soviets wrought. In one night the Russians destroyed the dozen beehives, the small animals all somehow disappeared, and a young German I had known nearby was executed. They imprisoned Father for years.

What was to happen with the abandoned homes and farms, with the fields almost ready for harvest? The advancing Soviets destroyed everything in their path, even the animals. Mercifully, perhaps, the farmers who fled did not have to witness the devastation, as they were no longer there. Only later did they learn that the fields were overgrown and uncared for, even during the following year's harvest, and their animals would again not have the necessary feed for the coming winter.

They later learned that "Sovietization" of the agriculture already began in 1946 in the form of land redistribution. The goal was complete collectivization. Land was seized from the owners and reallocated. If a farmer chose to remain on his land, ridiculously strict limits were imposed on the size of the land he was allowed to keep to feed his own family. It was never enough to maintain sustenance, nor even to still the hunger. In the end, collectivization succeeded in removing all incentive of each individual farmer, resulting in a steep drop in production.

During the summer of 2012, while paying a visit to my Jelgava cousins, the Uices, Ēriks Uice and I drove to the Dobele vicinity to see if we could find the homes of some of our ancestors. We did not have much luck. Many of them were destroyed and abandoned, the wood which had formed the walls of the homes had been looted for use as kindling. Those which still remained inhabited, notably Papus' family's home, Bākuļi, were occupied by Soviet squatters, still there from the pre-1991 era. At Jaunzemji where the home of

Mimmīte's grandmother's family had once stood, is a stone kolkhoz building with a proud Soviet sign, "In this building on November 20, 1946, eleven Šķibe district farmers united to form the first kolkhoz in Latvia – *'Nākotne.'*" The name, *"Nākotne,"* means "Future."

FOR A WHILE THAT SUMMER OF 1944, my cousins Stariņ and Daucis spent some time with us in Džūkste, where their mother had brought them for safety. She was a widow, a teacher in Jelgava, and sometimes could not look after them. Stariņ recalled that when he heard cannons blasting in Džūkste, he squirmed hurriedly under the kitchen table for safety. This incident that he so vividly remembered was as the Russian tanks rolled through the town. Latvian partisans threw grenades at them, and there were many injured, both Russians and Germans. The school building was designated an emergency clinic. Mrs. Baumanis, the region's doctor, ministered to the wounded from both sides, and Mimmīte was among those who helped. As there was no hospital in Džūkste, the sick and wounded were evacuated to Tukums some 30 km. away.

Bit by bit, as the Russians advanced and the Germans gave up ground, it became undeniable that our family had to decide on some action. Frightened, Mimmīte telephoned her sister Anniņa, at the time living in Līvbērze. Tētiņ could not abandon his postmaster duties, but Mimmīte wondered if she and her daughters could go stay with her. However, Anniņa explained that it was not possible, since she and her son Valdis were not staying either.

Mimmīte at the time was pregnant with her third baby. One day, she was sitting outside in the sun against a farmhouse wall, knitting a bright red sweater for me. Soviet soldiers drove up in a car, and one, taking his machine gun, laughed as he shot an arc of bullets around her. For the time being, Tētiņ was on an errand somewhere.

"You were saved because red is the color of Mother Russia!" shouted the Russian before proceeding on.

Frightened, Mimmīte grabbed Marutiņa and me, and we three ran to a farmer's home deep into the forest, a part of Džūkste called Ērģelnieki. We knew the people, as we had always gone there to get milk. The veterinary doctor, Rita Gāle's father, also lived in Ērģelnieki. Rita herself at that time was staying in Jelgava. The farmers did not object to our presence, as they knew that their situation would be the same in similar circumstances.The post office building was the first that the Russians took over. Later, when she was able, Mimmīte went back to get some things from our post office apartment. Russians, intercepting her, gruffly demanded who she was.

"I am just a servant," Mimmīte answered.

Suspecting a trap, they forced her to walk ahead of them, their guns drawn. If anyone would shoot, she would be hit first. Arriving at the apartment, Mimmīte found that the Soviets had soiled all of the rooms. They had scattered everything from the bureau drawers and filled these with excrement, even smearing the walls with the filth. The floorboards had been pried up in an attempt to reveal hidden treasure. They had killed her chickens by throwing them against the walls of the building. Seeing it all, Mimmīte had to weep in frustration. Her favorite books were in the home, and she did not want to abandon them. Mimmīte took what she could, bundled them up in her skirt, and holding it in front like a pouch, carried the books back to Ērģelnieki.

When Tētiņ returned, he was very alarmed at what had happened, and he contacted Ziņģi. Alīse asked her husband Pulkvedis Silenieks to fetch Mimmīte, Maruta, and myself and bring us to her farm. Mimmīte's sister Rita had been storing her expensive Persian carpet and her sewing machine with us, and Mimmīte was able to pack them up in the carriage as well.

At that time in this summer of 1944, Rita and her sons were already with Alīse at Ziņģi. The homestead, located in the Auri district some 36 km. south of Džūkste, still seemed to be somewhat out of the way and isolated from the fighting. On June 27, Rita had also taken Papus from his apartment on Plūdoņa street in Jelgava and brought him there. However, our grandmother Mamma was in the sanatorium in Tērvete, 21 km. south of Ziņģi, where she was hospitalized because of her asthma.

We all had at one time or another spent many a lovely day at Ziņģi. The three Bištēviņš sisters had earlier spent summers there helping in the fields, thus earning their family in Jelgava additional fruit and vegetables to last all year. Among the family pictures of happy times at Ziņģi are the ones taken during "*Vasaras Svētki*," the Summer Festival, celebrated each year the 50th day after Easter. In 1944 this happened to be May 28, my second birthday. We are seen standing there in the bright sunlight – the children dressed in crisp white outfits, the mothers in summer frocks. On one of the pictures, the five young cousins are lined up according to age, the first of many pictures taken of us in that formation.

We all seem to be happy and carefree there in our last pictures in Latvia.

It was at this time that the paths in all of our lives took a different turn. It was also the point at which Anniņa started her own flight on bicycle through the Latvian countryside, her three-year-old son Valdis nestled in a basket on her bicycle. Her sister-in-law Tamāra Sveķis accompanied her, also by bicycle.

The Šnores' (Rita and her sons, Stariņ and Daucis) last days in Latvia were spent at Ziņģi, where their life was comfortable and relatively worry-free. Even in the late summer of 1944 it seemed like a small peaceful haven where the war had somehow been left behind, though what was just beyond their view was the reality that they all would have liked to avoid. They would soon have to flee, and with that knowledge in mind, saved what they could for the inevitable. Spending anything for frivolities was out of the question. Still, the adults knew how to make a young boy's day special. Daucis, who celebrated his birthday at Ziņģi that summer on August 18, still remembers a very happy time, stating, "The chair was extremely nicely decorated with flowers for my fifth birthday celebration in Latvia in 1944."

STARIŅ SAID THAT IT WAS near the end of August that they all left Ziņģi in three horse-drawn carriages. The first one was occupied by the 54 year old Alīse, her 64-year old husband Pulkvedis Pēteris Silenieks, and Papus. The second was driven by Rita and included her sons and their family's belongings. The third carriage was used by the Kalniņš family – Antonija Kalniņš and her three sons – Tālivaldis, Imants, and Viesturs, the two younger ones about the same ages as Stariņ and Daucis. Mrs. Kalniņš was pregnant with her fourth baby. Her husband was not present with his family, as he had joined the German army and was fighting with the Latvian Legion. Until the flight, the Kalniņš family had been living and working in Ziņģi for about three years.

Stariņ said that it was very slow going. He would often descend from the carriage, walk a distance by foot with the Kalniņš boys, and then climb in again. The first night the refugees spent in the woods. Subsequent nights, if they were lucky, they were able to bed down on hay in barns. Many farms were already deserted, and if they were not, the farmers were forthcoming in aiding the travelers.

From Ziņģi, the three wagons first made their way to Tērvete, 20 km. south of Dobele. Mamma was a patient there in the Tērvete sanatorium, and they needed to get her for the flight. Approaching it, they unexpectedly came upon her at an intersection. She had been out walking, and so was simply taken along in the carriage for the journey. It seemed like a stroke of luck, meeting up with her there, as the flight could then continue without further delay.

Our family did not join the caravan. Mimmīte and Tētiņ were still undecided as to what we should do. Should Mimmīte with Maruta and me join the others and leave Tētiņ to finish his work, or should Tētiņ just abandon everything and accompany us on our flight? At that time, the utter permanence of any of our decisions was still not evident. Circumstances in Džūkste seemed to change now and again, as one day Germans seemed to have gained the upper hand, and the next day Russian soldiers were seen where the Germans had been. Tētiņ, as Postmaster of Džūkste, also wondered if his livelihood there was really coming to an end. If we left and then were to come back after all, would there still be a life for us in Džūkste? Toward the end of August, before the three-wagon caravan left Ziņģi, Mimmīte, Maruta, and I returned to Džūkste to be with Tētiņ.

LIEPĀJA, THE PORT CITY IN the southern corner of Latvia on the Baltic Sea, had a harbor from which it would be possible to board a ship for Germany. Ventspils, much farther to the north, was another. During the turbulence and confusion of the flight of Latvians from their homeland, many became separated from their families in one way or another. Some did not even know if their friends or family had already started their flight, and if they had, were they headed for Liepāja or for Ventspils? Many had found it necessary to flee on the spur of the moment, without being able to contact their loved ones. Under these circumstances, it was not surprising at all that they lost touch with one another in the ensuing chaos. The region's newspapers recognized the need and provided a means of communication in an effort to reunite the refugees with their families. Every edition had a column in which refugees could place requests for information which might lead to reunion.

The following ad appeared in the August 25th edition of the newspaper *Kurzemes Vārds*:

> News is requested of my sisters, Lidija Neimanis of the Džūkste post office and of Anna Sveķis of the Bērzes home, "Kļaviņas," also of Bisenieka street 28-3. Please send notice to Folk Aid in Kuldīga to the attention of Margarita

Šnore, neé Bištēviņš, of Jelgava, Bisenieka street 28-3, or of Auri district, "Ziņģi."

At the time of the ad's placement, Rita had probably not yet arrived in Kuldīga, but she was most certainly on her way. Whether heading for Liepāja or Ventspils, refugees would have to pass through Kuldīga. Perhaps Rita's ad already elicited a response from Anniņa, because the next ad, again in *Kurzemes Vārds,* appeared on September 2 and requested information of only one sister: "Searching for my relative, Lidija Neimanis of the Džūkste post office."

AS THE SITUATION IN DŽŪKSTE worsened, it brought the undeniable realization that, indeed, we had to leave. Though we held out hope that circumstances would not come to this, events did not change in our favor and we thought of the danger that we all had faced during the previous Soviet occupation. The time to leave was imminent, while the Soviets were still occupied with fighting the Germans, rather than annihilating the Latvian population.

Mimmīte had seen the newspaper ads that Rita had placed in *Kurzemes Vārds*, and she and Tētiņ decided that he would accompany us as far as Kuldīga and hope for a rendezvous with Rita's group there.

Photographs were few and they were taken along, as were clothes for the children. One took along only what could be carried. Among the valuables, presumably from Ziņģi, were some silver spoons which after our flight and immigration to America, are still with me now in Vermont. One is etched with the gothic letters LU, which could be for Lidija Uice,

Alīse Silenieks' sister-in-law, and a little one with EB, maybe a childhood spoon of our grandfather Eduards or his sister Elizabete "Lisetti" Bištēviņš, Alīse's mother. These could be used for barter to pay for goods during the flight, as there was no money to purchase anything. Some silver items were indeed exchanged for goods or services. Maruta added that eventually in Haunstetten, a couple of the spoons were melted down to form the ornate brooches which Latvians, in this case, Maruta and I, wore on our national costumes. Unfortunately, the books about which Mimmīte had cared so much had to be left behind.

Kārlis Renga, a friend in Džūkste, lent Tētiņ a horse and carriage, and with this he was able to be with us as far as Kuldīga. We had left in the darkness of night, because if detected in daylight, we could have been shot. The journey continued through nighttime until we were far from Soviet eyes. Tētiņ noted that on September 19, he accompanied us to Saldus. Rita, by then not having heard any news, was still worried about the whereabouts of Lidija and our family and we found still another ad in the newspaper *Tēvija* on September 19, the day that we reached Saldus: "Searching for relatives from Džūkste, Alfrēds Neimanis and family; from Džūkste Lidija Neimanis."

All roads were full of refugees in their carriages making their slow way to the harbor cities where they would be able to get onto a ship bound for Germany. The Folk Aid organization, taking note of the large number of refugees making their exhausting journey, decided to try to make it somewhat easier by establishing aid stations every 20 to 25 km. These had supplies of warm food and bread for the refugees and feed for their animals. Also available were the services of blacksmiths, who were able to repair broken wagon wheels and replace lost horseshoes.

Three days later, on September 22, we arrived in Kuldīga, and Mimmīte was reunited with her sisters Rita and Anniņa. Everyone in our party then sat down to try to determine what would be the best course of action. The town was already full of refugees looking desperately for a way out of Latvia. Kuldīga had been a logical rendezvous point that Rita had selected. It was in Kuldīga that the road came to a junction dividing it into two, each branch heading in a straight line either to Ventspils or to Liepāja, to one seaport or to the other. At this time our refugee group did not know which way they should go, but listening to radio news reports of the best possibilities at any particular time, they decided on Liepāja. The next day, having accompanied us to Kuldīga, Tētiņ returned to Džūkste and to his work with Kārlis Renga's horse and carriage. When things were resolved, he would rejoin us in Liepāja. Maruta and I stayed with Mimmīte and joined the caravan which consisted of the three horse-drawn carriages.

ON THE WAY TO LIEPĀJA, between Kuldīga and Aizpute lie seven villages once inhabited by a social and ethnic group of Latvians. These were the Curonian *Ķoniņi* (Kings), descendants of the area nobility having their own coats of arms and tracing their origins to the 14th century. The inhabitants were not peasants, but rather a special estate of freemen who possessed independent farms. They had historically escaped serfdom and were not the property of any medieval lord, as the other farmers in Latvia were. In fact they enjoyed privileges, such as hunting and fishing rights. These privileges were lost in 1929, when the Latvian Parliament decreed that the villages should become single farmsteads. With time, the farmsteads have been abandoned, and the families have dispersed.

Stariņ relates that on our way to Liepāja, we came upon one of the Curonian villages, Viesalgas, near the town Venta not far from Kuldīga. The family was headed by the retired General Mārtiņš Peniķis, a colleague of Pulkvedis Silenieks. General Peniķis invited our group to stay at Viesalgas for one or two nights.

Maruta told me a lively memory of what could have, or not, happened during our time in Viesalgas:

> I must have been considered more grown-up than I really was (four years old). That we were in flight-mode was impressed upon me. When we got to the house near the woods, I was taken to my room, with a window looking out onto a pretty, leafy scene. Almost immediately, I was put to bed. There I lay, alone, not knowing where you or Mimmīte were. And not knowing either how to get out to potty. Early that morning, I was awakened by what sounded to me like hunting horns, full-throated and mellifluous. Later, a lady came in to rouse me – I was awake, of course, and heading out of the room. She cried out when she saw the wet sheet. This was very embarrassing, especially since it was a decision on my part to wet the bed and no longer possible to blame it on my babyhood.

THROUGHOUT OUR FLIGHT, we were continuously within a throng of refugees. In one of the towns to which we came,

Kazdanga, the old 1876 school building was temporarily equipped with makeshift bedding for refugees for the night. Imants Kalniņš has another memory of Kazdanga. He said that this is where he and the boys rolled dry leaves into paper and tried smoking them.

Arriving in the vicinity of Liepāja, we encountered crowds with the same intent as ours and had to endure a long wait before we could get anywhere near a ship. It was not just a matter of arriving in Liepāja and heading for the harbor. A certain amount of organization had to take place to avoid the chaos and confusion generated by the enormous number of refugees. A way-station had been set up in Kapsēde, about 10 km. north of Liepāja. There everyone was required to register upon producing a passport or personal identity card. This was executed in the order of the arrival of each refugee, and those registered were issued numbers reflecting the sequence.

Here too, in the Kapsēde camp, the refugees were cared for by the Folk Aid organization. Besides providing them with hot meals, Folk Aid made available the services of doctors and first aid stations. The German army provided buildings for the women and children to sleep, though the men had to fend for themselves. Cots were also set up in the railroad station for refugees to spend the night. One of the town's saunas was made available for use at no cost on Saturdays.

A town secretary from a farming community had managed to take along unused passports. These he readied for refugees who did not have any or had lost them. If men were found to not be in possession of passports, they could be subjected to conscription elsewhere. It was not unusual that refugees came to the aid of each other in this and other ways in their time of need.

For the refugees' benefit, *ad hoc* organizations were established. Young ladies of the area organized a place for children to be cared for while their parents busied themselves in organizing shelters and other necessities. Throughout the day, radio broadcasts brought the news in fifteen-minute intervals in both the Latvian and Lithuanian languages. The broadcasts were interspersed with pleasant musical interludes.

Newspapers were available to keep everyone up to date with whatever was happening regarding the war. For those still without news of their loved ones, they provided another opportunity for a search leading to a possible reunion. Refugees were also alerted to the suggestion that upon reaching Germany, they should fill out cards with their identity, whereabouts, and intended route. These cards would be sent to Berlin for the purpose of establishing a registry enabling separated family members to later receive information of each other's possible whereabouts.

After a few days those refugees who were registered were sorted into groups, and when the time came each group was escorted to the port of Liepāja. Only those registered in Kapsēde were allowed to enter the city. Once there, refugees had to apply for a ship's boarding card. Immediately after receipt of the cards, they were to make their way to the assigned ship and commence to board.

A maximum of 100 kg. of personal items was allowed but absolutely no furniture. As some refugees had packed too much while others had nothing, attempts were made to rally the generosity of those having a surplus, while at the same time discouraging profiteering. It was advised that horses could be given to the army, for which the refugees would be well compensated. Any cows or oxen were to be delivered to the city's central meat plant.

THE KALNIŅŠ FAMILY ALONG with Alīse and Pulkvedis Silenieks, most probably managed to find room on a ship headed for Germany earlier than the rest of us. At any rate, neither Stariņ nor Imants Kalniņš remember each other after Liepāja until we all somehow ended up in the same DP camp much later in Haunstetten. Imants related that the presence of Pulkvedis Silenieks was beneficial to them on at least one other occasion during their flight. They were in Marienbad (Mariánské Lázně) when the Pulkvedis was somehow able to acquire a car and driver who drove them to the Czech-German border.

On September 29, Tētiņ made his way from Džūkste to Kapsēde to be with us once more. At the time, we still had not received our permission to proceed on to Liepāja. There was no news as to when we would be able to board a ship for evacuation to Germany. Many refugees who had reached Liepāja before us were already waiting. The ships arriving and leaving were very few, and when they set sail, they did so full of wounded German soldiers. If there was room, it was then allotted to the refugees. Before he returned once more to Džūkste, Tētiņ gathered his family to him, and taking little snips of our hair, folded the three precious mementos into a small piece of paper, and kept these very close to him.

TĒTIŅ'S SISTER EDĪTE NEIMANIS at the time 32 years old, worked as a physician at the Ķemeri resort, some 44 km. west of Rīga. Since its opening in 1936, the luxurious Ķemeri hotel was visited by those rich enough who came for treatments of the healing mud baths and sulfurous springs to restore their nerves, their bones, joints, and muscles to health once more. As the hotel's doctor, Edite had the use of a Mercedes to ferry her to and from her various patients. When the Russians arrived, they seized the Mercedes "for use," she was told. They gave Edīte a paper receipt saying that she will shortly be receiving payment for it. Needless to say, no payment was ever forthcoming.

I have a picture of Edite with "Mammucītis," Tētiņ's 66-year old mother, our grandmother Marija Neimanis, who was visiting Ķemeri in the fall of 1944. She had come from Valmiera because Edīte was to be married in the next few days. They are sitting on a bench on the Ķemeri grounds, both smiling pleasantly, and when Edīte and I spoke about the picture, she said she remembers the flowery dress she is wearing as if it were yesterday.

"Do not be fooled by our happy faces," she said. "This was a time of extremely great anxiety for us. Within a day or two, we also started our flight from Latvia. "

On September 24, 1944, in the Rīga Dom, Edīte married the 38-year old Jānis Platais, an economist from Vecpiebalga in eastern Latvia.

Tētiņ, Maruta, and Pappucītis in Džūkste

At Ziņģi with Alīse

May 28, 1944. Our last pictures taken in Latvia, at Ziņģi.
Lidija, Anna, Rita, with children
Maruta and Dagnija, Valdis, Daucis, and Stariņ

Five cousins

Edīte and her Mercedes at Ķemeri

Edīte and Jānis Platais' wedding, September 24, 1944

2nd row: Marta Neimanis, 5th from left is Mammucītis, 6th Jānis'sister, Ina Meisters.

3rd row: 4th from left, Andrejs Neimanis

CHAPTER THREE

ANNIŅA'S FLIGHT

Mimmītes's younger sister Anna Svekis was not in the caravan from Ziņģi as it made its slow journey that summer. She was reunited with the others in our group later in Kuldīga. Her own flight had already commenced much earlier.

Anniņa, with her big round eyes, was undeniably the most beautiful of the siblings. Mimmīte said that as a child Anniņa was very cheerful and was always singing, which seemed to raise everyone's spirits. In 1940 she married a fellow teacher from Jelgava, Juris Sveķis. Their son Valdis was born in April 1941 in Bauska where the family lived at the time. 1941 was the "Year of Horror," the year that the Soviets conducted the mass deportations to Siberia during

May and June. At the time, fellow teachers had already warned her, "You have to leave right away! You are going to be on the next train to Siberia!" A frightening possibility, and having been warned, she imagined terror looming around every corner. Anniņa – ever vigilant, often read more into what she observed than what was actually there. Until then, any benign event would startle her into unreasonable fright. Not only the explicit warnings she received, but her own fearful observations convinced her of her unavoidably imminent exile.

One day, riding in a bus, she observed a motorcyclist traveling next to it at the same speed. The rider seemed to be glancing more often than necessary at the bus, as if searching for someone through the dusty windows. "He's searching for me!" she thought. "He is the enemy, and he is looking for me." Anna was certain of it. She immediately associated his presence with the warnings she had received and became mistrustful of everything and everyone.

One of her duties as teacher was to take the children for a walk every morning. Nearing a house close to the school, she heard a voice calling pleadingly from its basement.

"Dear Latvians, please help! Please help, dear Latvians!"

Later she discovered that a man was imprisoned there – another teacher – and that he was being tortured. However, there was nothing that she or anyone else could do to help him. The next day Anna changed the route of the children's walk in order to avoid the pitiful house.

In April of 1942, when Valdis was 11 months old, Anna's husband volunteered to fight against the Communists and he joined the German forces. After a two-month training period in Austria where the men could still celebrate the Latvian mid-summer festival Jāņi, they were sent by train to the front. He had hoped to be part of a Latvian Legion regiment. Though there were Latvians in his company, once at the front, the men were distributed into groups having very few Latvians in each. Thus they became a part of the German war machine, and as such, were nothing more than pawns in foreign dress fighting for an alien power under a strange flag. There was nothing that they could do. Any attempt to evade the obvious would mean wartime military court.

This was the German Alpine troop of the 1st Mountain Division, the rifleman company which fought in the second battle of Kharkov and then participated in the offensive through southern Russia and into the Caucasus near Stalingrad. The battle Operation Edelweiss was named after the embroidered insignia on the soldiers' sleeves. In these battles of Operation Barbarossa, Hitler wanted to capture the Caucasus oil fields in the campaign codenamed Case Blue, commencing at the end of June that year. However, the German forces suffered defeat at Stalingrad and were forced to withdraw from the region.

Juris had enlisted in the spring of 1942, and already in September there was no more news of him. It had to be presumed that he had already fallen. Anniņa had only one photograph of her husband in his German military uniform. Afraid that she and Valdis could one day fall into Soviet hands, she snipped the uniform from the picture, leaving only her husband's face. She could not risk the discovery by the Soviets that she had been married to a member of the German forces.

None of the circumstances of her husband's death were known to her until some 40 years later. It was in the 1980s that she happened to read an article in the Latvian newspaper *Laiks* written by Jānis Gulbītis, a fellow soldier who had served in the same company as Juris. Contacting the author, she finally discovered what had happened to her husband.

Stationed in the Caucasus, Gulbītis, Juris, and other men were on maneuvers. Gulbītis heard a shot ring out and saw Juris, near him, suddenly collapse. He hastened to his side, calling out to him. The only sound that Gulbītis heard from Juris was a weak moan. He saw that Juris was bleeding from his neck and chest, and he gestured to an aide for assistance. The medic immediately hurried to Juris' side. Gulbītis could only watch him pull the injured man down lower to where he was out of view of the enemy. He himself could not delay but had to continue on with the maneuver. Gulbītis lost contact with Juris and surmised that he was most probably taken to a nearby nursing station, though he mentioned that even medics were sometimes killed in battle.

Anniņa thought that if a nursing station were overrun by Soviets, they would not hesitate to execute the wounded. Nursing them to health was certainly not in their interest. Jānis Gulbītis was able to provide Anniņa with some photographs of Juris in the rifleman company, and she displayed these, enlarged, on the walls of her apartment.

AFTER HER HUSBAND'S ENLISTMENT in 1942, Anniņa continued her work as a teacher. Later she took Valdis and left Bauska to return to Jelgava where Papus and Mamma lived. There she rented an apartment, and her mother-in-law, also in Jelgava, tended to her grandson during the day. So passed another two years until the summer of 1944 and the return of the Russians.

Wherever the Soviet troops surfaced, they continued their atrocities of torture, rape, and murder. From one woman they tried to discover the whereabouts of her husband. This she had no way of knowing, and she pleaded with them, "I don't know! Please believe me!" Not convinced, they seized her arms and forced her to watch as they poured boiling water over her baby. After that, the child's mother lost her mind. There were numerous happenings such as this, and when there was no escape only suicide seemed to offer relief. Latvians, besieged and desperate, waited with hope that the Allies would somehow realize their need and come to Latvia's aid against the Soviets, but of course, no help came. It was incomprehensible to them that the Americans and the Soviets were both allied forces.

As early as July 1944, Anna had made her decision to flee. She made an initial attempt at flight by bicycle from Jelgava to Līvberze in the Bērze district some 14 km. westward. Her three year old son Valdis was nestled in the bicycle basket. Along the way, here and there she observed Soviet soldiers in the distance. At such times she hid with Valdis in the bushes. When the soldiers had gone, Anna again decided to return to the house in Līvbērze. Huddling there in the dark, she heard someone arrive on horseback and ask the neighbors where she was living. Anna had no idea whether this stranger was trying to help, but not wishing to find out, she decided to not stay any longer.

In a piano in her apartment in Jelgava Anna had hidden a revolver, and she resolved to get it. However, after about 10 km., Anna came face to face once more with Soviet tanks and abandoned that idea. Having again returned home, she and her sister-in-law Tamāra Sveķis made new plans. This time, the two women set out once more by bicycle with Valdis again in Anna's basket. This is how the three of them fled through Latvia during the next two months, Anna dressed in her summer dress. In one town, she was given a pair of mittens. She now had a summer dress and mittens, but was grateful even for these.

Their progress was slow as they rode from town to town, working here and there for food and a place to sleep. Along the route they met German soldiers who were also fleeing the Russians. Three-year old Valdis was exhausted, and the Germans sometimes took him into their wagon to lighten the women's load.

One night deep in a forest they discovered a small bungalow in the midst of German and Soviet crossfire, and there Anniņa did find a gun. Not knowing from which distance the gunfire was coming, she resolved that she had to be prepared. Hermanis had taught her and Rita the use of a firearm. In the darkness the women huddled, Anna holding the weapon ready, contemplating what she would have to do if the Soviets found them. With the morning light, the gunfire quieted, and once more they were able to continue on their journey. It seemed to her that throughout the fighting, the occupation of this part of Latvia had continually shifted back and forth between the Germans and the Soviets. Finally, selecting strategically timed periods during which to continue their flight, they arrived in Saldus.

When they reached the town, Anna and Tamāra obtained a shelter and placed ads in a newspaper to try to locate relatives who might be searching for them. The newspaper,

Kurzemes Vārds listed names that were registered with the Central Refugee Office in Liepāja. It also reported other news helpful for refugees making their way to the port city. The newspaper even listed letters which their office had received and which were destined for recipients who might be passing through. These letters were held for the addressees until claimed. News was also reported of the possibilities of travel from Liepāja to Rīga and back, either by ship or train, whether special permits for the journey were necessary, and the like. Margarita Šnore placed another ad requesting news of her sisters Lidija Neimanis and Anna Sveķis. It was through these ads that they were again reunited in Kuldīga, each seeing their names in the newspaper, seeking reunion with one another.

PART OF THIS STORY SEEMED to me quite improbable. How could anyone, much less two women and a child last for two months in a forest wilderness with only sporadic shelter from the weather, without provisions, clothing, food, and other necessities of life? A Sveķis cousin, Edgar Anderson, whose family fled from Jelgava at about the same time, recounted a similar experience:

> Literally hours before the Soviet bombing of Jelgava on July 27th, 1944, my father showed up at our home on 3 Post street with a horse drawn carriage, and we all set out within 20 minutes, my parents and I. We fled across the Kurzeme countryside until October 31, when my father succeeded in getting us onto a ship in Liepāja because the captain wanted the horse, for food, I assume. So it took us three months to flee from Latvia.

My cousin, Stariņ, agreed:

> It's quite possible that such a journey took several months. In July, while the front was still in Lithuania, several Soviet armored tank forces broke through and made it past Jelgava almost to the Gulf of Rīga. Everybody in Zemgale (Latvia's southwestern region) knew they had to leave. Once out of immediate danger, people seemed to want to take their time, hoping for good news, because nobody really wanted to leave Latvia.

2nd from left in transport, facing forward,Juris Sveķis, in the German Alpine troops in 1942.

Anna and Juris Sveķis

Margarita and Austars Šnore

At Ziņģi
Standing: Stariņ, Valdis, Daucis, last three are Viesturs, Imants, and Tālivaldis Kalniņš. Maruta and Dagnija are in front.

CHAPTER FOUR

THE FERRY, *M/S PETER WESSEL*

We had already reached the Liepāja vicinity on September 29, as Tētiņ stated in his notes. He had hitched a ride and visited us that morning, but later again returned to Džūkste. It would be another ten days before our group could board any ship, so an often nervous period of waiting in Kapsēde commenced. Some refugees who had managed to take their horses and other animals left them there, abandoned. The poor beasts waited patiently for their masters to return until they were claimed by anyone who saw a use for them.

The waiting for us finally came to an end as the *M/S Peter Wessel* slowly pulled into port. Before the war, she had served as a Norwegian ferry operating between Larvik in southern Norway and Frederikshaven, Denmark. After Norway surrendered to Nazi Germany, the Germans immediately commandeered the ship, taking it out of its ordinary ferry route in April 1940. The *M/S Peter Wessel* remained under German control until the end of the war in Europe in May 1945. During this time she was used to ferry injured German soldiers back to Germany, and if there was room, took on refugees eager to escape from Latvia. Stariņ remembers that the *M/S Peter Wessel* had comfortable upholstered seats, a luxury on simple ferries.

The evening before our departure, we went for a last walk along the coast of Liepāja. Anniņa related that I had wanted to walk in the water, straining at the adult hands that were holding me back, and Marutiņa started crying, "Daģītis will fall into the big bowl!" The sea had been very choppy that day.

So it was that the next morning, October 8, 1944, we left Latvia on the *M/S Peter Wessel*. There was a general feeling of relief, but one can imagine the emotions of the refugees as they stood on the deck of the ship, watching the coast gradually turn into a sliver of what had been their Latvian homeland and then disappear completely as it met the distant morning mist. Standing on the deck a few voices mournfully sang the Latvian national anthem, *"Dievs, svētī Latviju"* (God bless Latvia). It was a sorrowful goodbye. We were not sure where we were going or what the future held for us. We only knew that we were leaving Latvia, joining thousands of other refugees without homes and without homelands. We were no longer in charge of our own destinies, but were subject to whatever benevolence we could receive through the good will of others.

When Tētiņ finally made his own trip to Liepāja on October 26, he found our names registered in the *M/S Peter Wessel* ship's manifest on October 9. So he knew that we all had indeed embarked and that our ship had set sail.

Mimmīte had managed to take along some food – fish, bacon, and honey, but this was stolen on the ship. Everyone, the refugees and the German soldiers, they all were hungry.

The Soviets tried to bomb the *M/S Peter Wessel* along the way and the ship shook and floundered but somehow we avoided being hit. We seemed to have God's protection, as many other ships did go down from being torpedoed and bombarded.

Anniņa told the story of the flight of a school friend of Mimmīte, a woman named Mērija, who with her two daughters embarked on another ship leaving Liepāja. Her husband had been a magistrate in Latvia. It was his idea for Mērija and himself to travel on separate ships so that they both would not be lost. They did not want the children left alone in case of a disaster. They would find a way to meet up later. He and the son left, and she and the girls waited for another ship. Unfortunately the ship carrying Mērija and her daughters did not escape attack. The bombs found their mark and the seas swallowed it up. Rescuers were able to save Mērija, but one of the girls disappeared in the swirling waters and the other child drowned in her mother's arms. Reunited with her husband, Mērija thereafter could not tolerate the sight of him and they eventually divorced. She went to live in Texas and later died there of cancer. He settled in Grand Rapids in the early 1950s where other Latvians, also Anniņa, lived.

One other family with young children was scheduled to depart Latvia the next day. They were from Liepāja and therefore near enough to receive the news firsthand of how each ship fared on the voyage. They listened in horror to the report of how one ship sailing the day before their own scheduled departure had been torpedoed. It sank with all refugees and wounded soldiers on board. The parents had to search deep within their consciences. There seemed to be a strong possibility of the family losing their lives at sea. The alternative was to stay in Latvia and be sent to an almost certain death in Siberia. Sadly they decided to stay.

Our own voyage on the M/S Peter Wessel took two days, and we eventually reached Danzig (Gdansk in Poland) on October 10, but remained on board until Gotenhafen (Gdynia) some 13 km. farther west.

OUR AGES AT THE TIME of our flight from Latvia:
Eduards Bištēviņš, "Papus," 74
Marta Bištēviņš, "Mamma," 57
Alfrēds Neimanis, "Tētiņ," 37
Margarita Šnore, "Rita," 34
Tamāra Sveķis (Anna's sister-in-law), 32
Lidija Neimanis, "Mimmīte," 30
Anna Sveķis, "Anniņa," 27
Austars Šnore, "Stariņ," 8
Daumants Šnore, "Daucis," 5
Maruta Neimanis, "Marutiņa," 4
Valdis Sveķis, 3
Dagnija Neimanis, "Daģītis," 2.

The Soviets made their final move on Rīga and captured it by October 13, 1944. For all of us, then, the flight seemed to have taken place at the last possible moment. Thus started for us, those fortunate enough to have escaped, a 46-year period of exile in strange lands which in time became our adopted homelands. There we grew up, and there we prospered. But for those left behind, one could say that there started a 46-year period of exile within their own homeland of Latvia.

The harbor in Liepāja, Latvia

The ferry *M/S Peter Wessel*

CHAPTER FIVE

TĒTIŅ'S SEARCH FOR US

The Soviet army had reached the Baltic Sea near Memel in Lithuania on October 10, thereby cutting off the German army's land route. Realizing that the attention of the world was being focused elsewhere, Stalin put his own agenda into play, and his armies made their measured, though unstoppable, way westward. After the capture of Rīga on October 13, the Soviets marched on to Kurzeme and cornered the German army, some 200,000 strong, which included the Latvian Legion soldiers. Trapped between the Baltic Sea and the Soviet front, they were in effect separated from the rest of the German armies. Realizing this, the German generals urged Hitler to withdraw. However, he still entertained a delusion of victory and denied his troops the opportunity of pulling out.

From mid-October, 32 German divisions and 20,000 men of the Latvian 19th Division were cut off from the rest of the German army and encircled from the east and south by the Soviets in the "Courland Pocket," including the battles in and around Džūkste. To the north and west was the Baltic Sea. Among the Latvian 19th Division soldiers, until his injury forced his evacuation to Germany, was my 33-year old uncle Hermanis Bištēviņš.

Six major battles were fought in what became known as the Courland Cauldron between October 12, 1944, and April 3, 1945. Throughout these battles, the defending legionnaires and the German forces fought on and remained undefeated. Together they managed to keep the Soviets out of Kurzeme until the very end of the war in Europe, when Germany finally capitulated on May 8. The presence in the area of the German army divisions and of our Latvian Legion was the major reason why it was still possible for us and so many other Latvians to escape during the fall of 1944, as the ships which evacuated the injured German soldiers also took on the fleeing Latvians.

We were among the 40,000 refugees who left Liepāja by ship to arrive in Gotenhafen. Another 8500 departed from Ventspils, and 34,000 left Rīga to sail to the Danzig port. Some 20,000 others fled over land. The number of Latvians seeking sanctuary in Germany totaled about 102,500. Had the Soviets been enabled to take control of Kurzeme earlier, none of these refugees would have been able to leave.

The fifth battle of the Courland Cauldron commenced on February 12, 1945, with a Soviet advance against the Germans at our home town of Džūkste. By February 16, the Germans there were vanquished and on the run. It was then that they decided to demolish the ancient Džūkste church, which had been built in 1689.

HAVING RETURNED TO DŽŪKSTE from Liepāja at the end of September, Tētiņ discovered that the other workers had abandonded their posts, and he found himself alone in the Džūkste post office. He finally received permission from the occupying German government to liquidate the post, which he did on October 14. He took the post office money and insignia, and as instructed by the German authorities made his way to Tukums and surrendered them there at the general Post Office. Though he could have left everything in Džūkste, he felt compelled to bring his job to completion. His work ethic was irreproachable.

Whether in the circumstances of the time, his was a good choice or not may be debatable, but there was no doubt in his mind. In retrospect his action was criticized by some who were less than kind. In truth, the only person who had any right to be critical was my mother. It was her side and presence that my father had left in order to finish his job, and I have not once heard a word of reproach from her lips. Whether soldier or partisan or civilian, everyone worked to try to sustain his land and livelihood as well as he was able, each in his own way.

Leaving Tukums, Tetin found that the war front was continually changing and expanding and he had to adjust his route from day to day. From Tukums on October 14 he made his way to Kabīle, then on to Kuldīga and to Klostere, a small town in the Turlava district. At the time Tētiņ remained oblivious to the fact that he was passing through the very area that was witnessing the intense fighting that would become known as the Courland Cauldron battles.

In Klostere, Tētiņ was pleasantly surprised to come upon his sister Edīte, their mother Mammucītis, and Edīte's husband, all of whom by then were also making their way to the coast as refugees. Jānis told him that while still in Rīga he had tried to send a car to Valmiera to pick up Pappucītis. Unfortunately it was forced to turn back, as the Soviet front had by then expanded and the road to Valmiera was not traversable. Pappucītis never knew about Jānis' effort, and for the rest of his life he wondered if he had been purposely abandoned. Tētiņ's father died in 1955 before it was possible to establish a reliable means of personal communication from the U.S.A. to Latvia.

From Klostere, Tētiņ left for Liepāja, and arriving there he discovered that Mimmīte, their daughters, Rita and Anniņa's families, along with the Bištēviņš parents were registered as passengers on the ship's manifest of the *M/S Peter Wessel* and had departed for Germany on October 8. Tētiņ himself was not able to board a ship until October 26, when the *Roedenbeck* set sail for Danzig. The *Roedenbeck*, like the *M/S Peter Wessel*, delivered weapons and munitions from Germany to Liepāja. For the return trip it took on wounded German soldiers, and if room allowed, of course refugees. Tētiņ wanted to rejoin his family as soon as possible, but they were already some 20 days ahead of him by now. Ships were faster than trains, but the journey was much more risky.

Late during the night of October 27, the *Roedenbeck* arrived in Danzig, but Tētiņ remained on board to disembark in Gotenhafen. Trains there already waited at the docks, as if to anticipate carrying refugees farther inland through Poland and then on to Germany. As usual, they were overfilled beyond capacity, but fortunately there were no officers to demand the presentation of either tickets or passports. It would have been chaos if these had to be checked and controlled. Tētiņ boarded a train to Gera from where his journey took him on to the Nussdorf camp for a stay at Haus Emden. On November 14 he was able to travel to Litzmanstadt (Lodz) and later on to Schneidemühle (now Pila in Poland). He was exhausted and hungry from his hurried flight. However, as he observed the blank look of exhausted indifference on the faces of his fellow travelers, he realized that they too had not rested for many days.

Litzmanstadt seemed to be a transit point for many refugees, and local townspeople gathered at its railroad station and ladled soup from their kettles, offering it to the new arrivals. On November 18 in Litzmanstadt, an old woman offered Tētiņ some pea soup, saying, "You have most probably not eaten for quite a while." For many of them and of course for Tētiņ, this was probably their first real nourishment in days.

As he was telling me this story, I thought how quaint and how trivial that Tētiņ would mention the offered pea soup at all. He not only described his pleasure in eating it, but even attributed to this event so much importance as to even write it in his notebook. Actually, as I learned much later, pea soup had a special place in every Latvian refugee's heart. It was so bland and so frequently offered that it became known as *"zaļās briesmas,"* the green horror. Not only pea soup, but this became true of many a refugee camp culinary offering. As any food staple became available, it was offered in such large quantities that in order to avoid its becoming spoiled, it remained on the menu until completely depleted. Perhaps the old woman who offered Tētiņ the soup was happy to see that at least somebody ate it so willingly. Though many DPs later swore that they would never look at pea soup again, Tētiņ in his later life never shied away from it. Perhaps he remembered the welcome relief from hunger that this soup had provided so long ago.

In Litzmanstadt, he discovered that a number of Latvian refugees had already passed through and had since departed. This area was still within the German enclave, and Tētiņ said that everywhere people greeted each other with a resounding *"Heil, Hitler!"* On November 22 he made his way to Neumühle. Rita, while still in Liepāja, had told him that it would be to Neumühle that we all would be heading, as she had a friend there. However, once in Neumühle, Tētiņ found no sign of us.

In the same way that the newspapers in Latvia had provided the refugees with information of the whereabouts of their family members and loved ones, in Germany it was the bulletin boards. These were set up in places where refugees happened to pass through or congregate, most often inside or near train stations. There it was also possible to leave a note on a scrap of paper tacked onto the board seeking information or to find an answer on one already posted. Refugees traveling through often indicated the direction they would be following or the next camp to which they would be heading.

Leaving Neumühle Tētiņ made his way to Plauen in eastern Germany, a distance of some 500 km. It was there that he discovered that our group had already passed through earlier and had left for Aussig in the Sudetenland part of Czechoslovakia. Arriving in Aussig on November 24, Tētiņ again searched out the bulletin boards and discovered that we had moved on to Podsedice.

CHAPTER SIX

GERMANY AND GERMAN-OCCUPIED POLAND

Historically, typhus had always made an appearance during periods when people were crowded together in unsanitary conditions complicated by hunger and poverty. The bacterium causing the illness is carried by lice or other insects and spread human to human by rodents or other animals. Untreated, typhus could kill about half of the people it infects. It appeared in epidemic proportions in Europe during World War II, understandably most particularly in concentration camps, but also among refugees and displaced persons, commonly known as DPs. In order to try to prevent the propagation of typhus, the vector of this disease, the body louse, had to be eliminated.

Though an effective vaccine had been developed during the war, its use for the prevention of typhus did not become available until much later. In the interim, the powerful and long-lasting pesticide DDT was utilized wherever possible, including at many a crossroad through which our group of refugees wandered. The adult lice would feed upon the host's blood, and the eggs would be laid and would attach themselves to the body's hair shafts. Even after having been blasted with a DDT-containing powder gun in one camp, if we happened to travel on to another one, we would again be deloused with still another dose of the noxious powder. It was not until much later that the world became aware of the health concerns posed by DDT, so it remained in use in agricultural applications at that time and even for years following the end of the war.

Stariņ's only vivid memory of Gotenhaven is of being deloused on the evening of our arrival. This consisted of every part of one's body with any hair being sprayed with the DDT. Because he was still young enough, he was allowed to go through the procedure with the women. Afterwards they all could shower. Anniņa said that at some camps we were also x-rayed. Perhaps the DDT and the x-rays were very injurious to the unborn baby Mimmīte was carrying, but there was no use protesting against any of the procedures.

Stariņ's reminiscences:

We stayed in Gotenhaven for another day or two before being sent by train to Posen (Poznan). The camp in

Posen (actually near Posen, as we never saw the city) must have originally been a POW camp. It was fairly large, with guard towers at the entrance and at corners in the fence. The wire fence was quite high with barbed wire along its top. A wire ran along the inside, two to three feet above the ground and 20 to 30 feet from the fence. Signs stating that anybody crossing the wire could be shot were suspended from it. One of the Latvians said that the people in the towers were Poles. We lived in the common single-story plywood buildings known in Latvian as "*barakas.*" Sleeping was in three-level bunks made of unfinished boards.

The most impressive thing about the camp was the sanitation facilities. The latrine for the camp was a room about 50 feet by 50 feet. I only saw the one for men. I assume the women's one was similar, on the other side of the back wall. There were about four shallow gutter-like depressions in the concrete floor with drop inlets, covered with pieces of shiny metal grid, apparently leading to an underground piping system. Along the gutters at five to ten foot intervals were 12 to 18 inch square pedestals about four inches high. Periodically, a fire hose was used to flush the system. Immediately adjacent to the building was a pond of black liquid, about 100 feet in diameter, where the effluent collected. I really did not notice a bad smell coming from it. A few times it was my task to take my blind grandfather over to the latrine. I took him to the door, which was the width of a garage door and at that time of year kept open all day. At the door an adult took over for me while I waited outside.

After about a week in Posen, we were sent to Neumünster, where we stayed for a few weeks, about 50 miles south of the Danish border. The beds in these barracks were only two-level and there were no towers. Somebody had cut an opening in the wire mesh fence and we were able to walk around outside the camp, but we had to stay inconspicuous…

From the camp at Neumünster, we went by passenger train to what is now the Czech Republic. I don't know why and who determined that we would go there. Along the way we stopped overnight at "camps" (groups of rooms with beds and food being provided) for refugees. The first one was very crowded. The number of refugees was so great that one bed was assigned per two persons. This was all right for my brother and me, but my mother was assigned to a bed where the other user was a Latvian man. Fortunately he had to leave around midnight, and they reached an agreement whereby he would have the bed until then and she would afterwards.

At the second stop, there were no accommodations for foreigners, and we were told to stay overnight at a camp for German refugees in the general area of Plauen. What a contrast! Instead of the usual kohlrabi soup, we received smoked eel, an expensive and highly prized delicacy even in peacetime Europe. Later that night we spent some time in an air-raid shelter, listening to falling bombs. Our stay in Plauen was only for a day or two.

AT THAT TIME GERMANY was full of refugees, not only German, but of many nationalities. Refugee services were already there for the new arrivals. No proof of national or political affiliation was requested, and somehow there was room for all of us.

At one of these camps, definitely not the one in the Plauen area, the requirement was that we all had to stand in line to get food. If you did not appear in person, you just did not get any. By this time, all of the children in our group were very pale and wasted, but especially Marutiņa seemed to be almost at the point of no return. Weakened by starvation and not having been seen by any doctor, she was so sick that she did not have the strength to get up from the bed. All she could do was vomit. Anniņa said that Marutiņa was like a little candle about to go out. In that camp during that week alone, eleven children had died. In order to get food, Mimmīte stood in the food line with Marutiņa cradled in her arms.

We realized very quickly that staying in that refugee camp would not be beneficial to any of us, especially the children. One after another they might get sick, and we had to avoid this at all costs. Transferring to another camp may not be an improvement, but nothing could be worse than where we were. Both Mamma and Rita spoke German very well. They approached the camp authorities and when granted an audience with the director, they claimed to have relatives living in Germany. "The family Schmitz, of München," they likely could have said. The director did not even give a second glance but just told them they were free to go. He was probably glad to get us out of his hair.

This brought us to another German camp where we didn't get any more food either, nothing really of substance, but the potatoes and porridge were a welcome addition. They had not been available in the previous camp. The children needed more nourishment, and Anniņa said she knitted sweaters at night so that she could trade them for milk. We did not stay at that camp for any length of time either.

At one camp we encountered drunken Russian soldiers. Not wanting to be confronted by them, the women tried to become invisible. Rita pleaded with her sister, "Anniņ, go hide somewhere." They threw some blankets over themselves so as not to be seen by the drunkards.

Not only from the Russians, but we also had to hide from the *Tieffieger*, the low-flying planes supposedly used by the Allies which sometimes strafed German civilians to demoralize them and to try to hasten their surrender. Some of these strafing incidents are what Maruta remembers:

> It is night and we're hunkered down in a ditch, waiting for the illuminating and the strafing bullets to stop so that we can be on our way again.
>
> "Mimmīt, what is happening?"
>
> "We're watching fireworks, dear."
>
> "But then, why is my bottom trembling?"

Traveling by rail, we sometimes had to vacate the train because Russians were taking over it for themselves. At such times, we all ran into the woods where we hid and waited for another train. When it came we jumped on and our flight continued. By this time, we had crossed the frontier into the Sudetenland.

Cousin Stariņ's story of the *Tieffieger:*

> Here is the story I promised with a *Reichsbahn* involvement. I don't know if you young'uns remember the *Tieffieger* (German noun, capitalized, plural same as singular, meaning deep flyer, deep in the ocean of air that surrounds us). They flew long-range USAF (maybe USAAC in those days) interceptors (US flew in the daytime, the Brits at night), usually escorting bombers. When not engaged in that, they went after targets of

opportunity on the ground. Among those were pedestrians and passengers of horse-drawn vehicles, who, within the borders of the German Reich (which included occupied territories) were considered the enemy. I was taught to "hit the dirt" when seeing a low-flying airplane. But I digress, the following are the events told to me by my mother.

Near the end of the war, we were living in the Sudetenland, so named because of a Sudetes mountain range nearby, a part of Czechoslovakia with a mixed Czech and German population that had been absorbed by Germany. The area we lived in was very close to the part of Czechoslovakia occupied by the Germans, but not incorporated into Germany proper, called at that time "*das Protektorat*" for short. The majority of the population in our area was Czech, which in our village became apparent only after the war, with people returning from camps or whatever. In the spring of 1945, with the Russians approaching, the Germans decided to move the inhabitants of a concentration camp (I found out, not too long ago, that our general area was home to quite a few concentration camps, among them well-known ones, but no death camps). These people were herded, under guard of course, on foot toward a then unknown destination. They "camped" for a night in a field of recently sprouted rape, the source of canola oil, and stripped it bare. The next day they were led through a neighboring town, when, as if a signal had been given, baked rolls *(Semmel)* started to rain on them. At the railroad station they were loaded unto flatcars to be transported to their destination.

The *Tiefflieger* pilots must have considered themselves to be really fortunate, seeing that large a group of the enemy, all crowded together, maybe even troops ...

(The 3 dots is an extremely popular Latvian literary device).

Imants Kalniņš also has a story somewhat reminiscent of Stariņ's *Tiefflieger* one. Their group was taking refuge in a village near Mariánské Lázně, where they had to walk through a wooded area to be able to get to the town. The Germans also used that same path to lead prisoners to their next destination, whatever that could have been. His mother saw that due to their weakeness, some of them were hardly able to keep up. She ran into the home, grabbed as many potatoes as she could carry, and gave them to those who seemed to be the weakest. Years later, when Imants asked his mother if she had no fear, as the Germans could have shot her, she replied, "Human beings need to help each other, no matter what it may cost."

CHAPTER SEVEN

PODSEDICE

November 5, 1944 through August 1945

Podsedice is a small town some 75 km. northwest of Prague in what in those days was Czechoslovakia. Historically, besides farming, the locals engaged in the mining of Bohemian garnet, at one time quite plentiful in the area. Podsedice was located in the Sudetenland part of the country. Unknown to us, it would be quite soon – within less than a year – and the end of the war, that the Sudetenland would be designated as being under Russian control.

Just some 19 km. to the northwest of Podsedice is Theresienstadt, a garrison city with an 18th century fortress. In 1940, the Gestapo adapted Theresienstadt to serve as a ghetto and concentration camp primarily for Jews from Czechoslovakia and others deported mainly from Germany and Austria. Some 33,000 people died there of malnutrition and disease. The ghetto and camp were still operating at the time that we arrived in Podsedice, and it was not until the end of the war that it finally closed.

Stariņ's story continues:

> Our next destination was Usti nad Labem (*Aussig an der Elbe*, if my German is correct), where we were to take a connecting train on the way to our destination, the village of Podsedice (*Podseditz* in German). My job while we were at the station was, as usual, to guard our luggage while the mothers, the sisters Rita, Lida (Lidija), and Anna took the little kids with them. I was eight at the time. My grandfather and grandmother were also traveling with us and must have gone with them as well, because I remember being all alone with the luggage. I don't remember the rest of the trip to Podsedice at all.
>
> Our camp in Podsedice consisted of two or more "modules". One, where our food was cooked, looked like it might have been a restaurant. Our module consisted of a room on the second floor of a building separating a yard with flanking stables and barns from the street. The farmer, whose last name was Anderle (a last name typical of Bavarians and Swiss), lived with his family on the first floor. German last names are common among Czechs. The Anderle's Czech ethnicity was affirmed by the nickname, pronounced Marzhenka, of their two or three year old daughter.
>
> The room we lived in was divided in two by a long table with about six two-level bunk beds on each side of it. There

may have been a couple of single level beds too. We were 20 to 25 people, all Latvians, of whom, as I remember, eight, including we, were children. At one end of the room there was a door to a storage room, about which my main recollection is that the long loaf of rye bread we periodically got was kept there under lock and key. It was my understanding that the door was kept locked so that the children would not eat up the bread all at once, but there may have been other reasons too. I don't know how long the loaf of bread was supposed to last, but I remember seeing a loaf once with one end green with mold.

Since we received our food from the camp, we did not have any ration cards. My mother said that the only food containing protein that was available in stores without ration cards was a salad made of finely chopped vegetables and snails with vinegar. It tasted quite good. We used mustard (it was very mild) to spread on the bread.

After the war was over, I remember going with Rita and Anna to steal peas in one of the fields outside the village. All three of us had knapsacks. Peas, having a large proportion of high-quality protein after ripening and drying, were the perfect dehydrated food for the German army. There were large fields of them, the plants being about six inches taller than me at that time. We filled our knapsacks and got back without anybody even noticing us.

There were even a few POWs living in that town with little apparent supervision. They were available for odd jobs. I remember the question, *"Brauchen Sie einen Franzosen?"* (Do you need a Frenchman?) After the war was over, I was among some other kids looking at the rooms that two of the POWs had lived in. By then they were a mess, with people trying to find something.

As Stariņ remarked, groups of refugees lived in separate locations with no evident control of them, but if considered as a unit, it could have been regarded as being a camp of quite some size. We took up residence in the Podsedice camp for displaced persons on November 5, 1944, and were immunized six days later. In my little immunization booklet is the notation that I was vaccinated on November 11 for diphtheria and scarlet fever and received booster shots on December 9. Of course vaccination benefitted everyone, as did using DDT to deter the spread of typhus. Our tight living circumstances required preventive methods to avoid catching and propagating any illnesses.

Mamma, because of the severity of her asthma, did not stay with us but had to be hospitalized in Aussig (Usti nad Labem).

IT HAD BEEN TWO MONTHS since we had last seen Tētiņ, and it was in Podsedice that we were finally reunited when he arrived on November 25. Tētiņ noted that the day after our reunion, he was able to buy 6 kg. of pears for 50 *Reichsmark*.

In most European towns linden trees graced the walkways and roads, but in the Sudetenland apple and pear trees seemed to be most plentiful. We were told that we could pick the fruit up from the ground, but plucking it from the trees was forbidden.

Once a young boy had climbed into a pear tree and was chided by an adult.

"Hey, there, what are you doing up in that tree?" the adult yelled.

"I'm making the pears fall down so that we are allowed to pick them up from the ground!" shouted down the boy.

Starin̨:

It was November when we got to Podsedice, but I was enrolled in the school (German) only in mid-April (1945). I went to the German school for about three weeks. All I remember about the school is the time that one of the kids came into the room without taking off his hat and some of the others started chanting: *"Einer Jude in die Stube! Einer Jude in die Stube* (A Jew in the room)!" Another thing I remember is that two girls from my class, Annemarie and Rosemarie, used to come to play with me (never both at the same time). I thought that Rosemarie was cute.

After the end of the war, I went to Czech school for about three months. They must have eliminated or shortened summer vacation to make up for time lost during the occupation. I remember my book *Ma prva ceska kniha* (My first Czech book). "r" and some other consonants are considered to be something like semi-vowels. Each day started with everybody standing next to their desk and singing the national anthem. I still remember the words and the melody, in a way.

There were a few times our mothers woke us up and took us to an air-raid shelter. I don't remember any bombs though. Even though the village was small, we had to be careful because some of the bombers had leftover bombs after bombing a city and they could drop them on communities (which had been warned by the Germans) that they crossed on their return flight. We saw the light from the bombing of Dresden on the horizon. I believe that the Brits' intent was to impress on the Russians their readiness to bomb anything so as to help dissuade them from barreling in their tanks across the North German plain past the agreed division line between the Soviet and the British zones. It would have been hard to motivate the Tommies (the British soldiers) to keep fighting after the war had been won. The Soviets, after their initial defeats against the Germans, found a fail-safe way of motivating. Their front-line troops were backed by NKVD (People's Commissariat for Internal Affairs, which was closely associated with the Soviet secret police.) obstruction battalions, whose job was to shoot those retreating or not advancing when ordered to do so, and who are said to have caused as many Soviet casualties as the Germans. For a while after the war, the Brits kept many German (and Latvian) POWs under conditions where their status could be quickly changed from POW to ally. Getting back to Dresden (figuratively speaking), it was not like it did not have any armament industry at all. A woman friend of Rita's was there in a concentration camp, working in an underground factory. She escaped during the bombing and managed to lie low until the end of the war.

I HAVE A LITTLE FRAGMENT of a notebook, onto which Mimmīte had made a sad little note in pencil, "*6 dec. piedz. meita.*" (December 6, daughter born) It was in Podsedice that Mimmīte went into labor and gave birth to a stillborn little girl on December 6, 1944, at 15:30. Mimmīte was aided by a midwife and Anniņa. A dead little baby is difficult to bring into the world, and Mimmīte had a very hard time of it. It didn't help that the midwife was crude and insulting. The next day, December 7, Tētiņ took the little body to a cemetery in the neighboring village of Dlaškovice, just a few miles away, and dug a little grave. There was no stone for a memorial, but he put up a tiny wooden cross. Tētiņ said that in those days, bodies were often buried where they died, sometimes even at roadsides.

When Marutiņa and I asked Mimmīte where the little promised baby was, Mimmīte said she had thought it over, and that she and Tētiņ were content with just the two of us. Anniņa considered that a very good answer, as we both were really too young to understand.

MARUTA, IN HER THEN 4-YEAR-OLD mind, had a fascination for the place where we lived in Podsedice. Thinking back to those days, she was convinced that we lived in a castle in Prague:

> We stayed there for a bit - perhaps a month or two. I liked our gloomy castle-like hostelry with the enclosed, stone-paved courtyard, a real castle with Palladian entrance gates. I have baroque horror memories of the place: the dead-stone grayness of the high walls, the hallway lined with crouching, springing, roaring taxidermy specimens, the hole in a wooden plank onto which I was placed to potty, the wind blowing cold air over my bottom, bringing on fantasies of falling through it and going down, down, down to the nasty moat below.
>
> In the camp I met a little boy who asked, *"Puņimāju pa ruski?"* the very first Russian that I ever understood.

Stariņ, our then 8-year-old cousin, being the only one left with an undeniable recollection of the circumstances of our escape from Latvia, set her straight:

That was Podsedice, not Prague.

Our mothers worked in fields about a mile from the village. The women were not paid for the work. Rita and Anna sold things like embroidered pieces of fabric that they had brought with them to get money for unforeseen expenses. The owner of the farm lived on the first floor, and we, together with about 20 other Latvians, lived in a large room on the second. The entrances to the stables for livestock opened onto the courtyard.

TĒTIŅ FOUND WORK IN LOVOSICE, a town 10 kilometers northeast of Podsedice. Because Lovosice was in the German occupied zone of the Sudetenland, many of its inhabitants left, and during the war only about 600 Czechs lived there. They were short of workers, and so it was that Tētiņ was able to find a job with the Germans. His first assignment on December 4 was to cut osier branches on the shores of the Elbe River. Osier is a type of fast-growing willow. When Tētiņ asked what they would be used for, he was told that they were needed by the war department for weaving baskets to carry and transport cannonballs.

Then from January 10 to May 8, 1945, Tētiņ was employed as a locomotive stoker for the *Deutsche Reichsbahn* in Lovosice. Part of his job was to maneuver the arriving trains onto the correct tracks for their destinations. Some trains ferried goods, others transported German soldiers, while still others contained Jews heading for destinations unknown.

The locomotive boss, Pfeiffinger, regularly sported a Nazi insignia. He now and then offered Tētiņ a pear which he then took home and gave to us. Also working on the train were a German, a Latvian, and the conductor, a Ukrainian. Tētiņ's job, besides stoking, was to ride with his head out of the train window as a lookout. When he questioned why and what he had to look for, as there was nothing to be seen, he was told that maybe someone would flag down the train in case the tracks were broken or had been bombed. This, Tētiņ said, never happened.

AT ONE STATION, A TRAIN was halted on an adjacent track, and on the platform next to it was a pile of luggage. Just as their train was leaving the station, the Ukrainian conductor from Tētiņ's train jumped out and grabbed a satchel from the pile, which, it turned out, was the property of a German soldier. As the train sped on its way, the conductor opened it. Inside there was not much, just a parachute and a loaf of bread. The Ukrainian offered Tētiņ some of the bread which he did not want to accept, but finally relented upon the conductor's insistence. Tētiņ put the rest of it inside his locker. The next day the bread was gone.

The conductor turned his attention to the parachute and scoffed. What good was this to anyone? He was about to toss it into the fire when Tētiņ stopped him. He'd take it, he said, and at the end of the day, he carried the chute home and gave it to a surprised Mimmīte. Together they unfurled it and stood wondering what they could possibly do with it. Nothing came to mind, so presently they rolled it up again and put it away into a corner of the room. I don't know at what point they actually made plans for it. At any rate, nothing was done until we reached the stability of our long sojourn in the

Haunstetten DP camp, where they finally made up their minds regarding its use, so I will return to that subject again later.

THE ADULTS IN PODSEDICE WERE required to work six days a week. Mimmīte was excused from manual labor at the beginning, as she was still not very well after giving birth to our stillborn little sister. So her duties were to look after the children, and Anniņa and Rita went to work. For their efforts they each got a slice of bread per day, said Anniņa. Russian soldiers or Czechs watched over them with rifles as they worked. The notion of a slice of bread per day is not an exaggeration. Bread and grains were in extremely short supply at that time. Stariņ said that they were treated like *Ostarbeiter*, slave workers who were brought in from the eastern provinces.

Tamāra had taken along some of her brother Juris' clothes from home. Anniņa put on the long baggy pants, tied the legs tightly around her ankles, and went to work. She gathered potatoes from the fields and hid some in the bulging sacks that the pants formed around her ankles. In the evening they cooked the five potatoes that she managed to hide, and each child got one potato for supper.

Stariņ continues:

> When spring came, which was earlier than in Latvia, our mothers worked in the fields. It was interesting that a crop was grown in fields containing apricot trees spaced in a regular pattern, about 30 feet in both directions. Another interesting thing was that the soil contained many little

pieces of garnet. I still have a small container full of them somewhere.

Valdis' comment:

I still have Annie's box of garnets. My only memory of Czechoslovakia is of the Russian army firing field artillery pieces into a farm pond to kill fish for food.

Daucis added:

Our mother, working in the orchard or the fields in the hot sun, had peeling sunburn blisters all over her shoulders as well as deeply cracked skin on her feet. She just accepted it as a part of life without complaining.

IT DIDN'T TAKE LONG FOR OUR refugee group to learn more about their surroundings and about that unique composition of the very earth from which they were harvesting the potatoes. Red garnets had been mined in the Bohemian Hills of Czechoslovakia since the 16th century, but the industry experienced a decline during the political and economic conditions of this era of our family's story. Still, the gems were there in the dirt, especially the area ten km. southwest of the town of Lovosice and also in the potato fields of Podsedice. Anniņa said that all anyone had to do was sift the sandy soil and the shiny pieces just fell out.

Picking up the little garnet nuggets was of course prohibited, but all of the potato harvesters did it anyway. Some hid them in their mouths behind their lips, but Anniņa and Rita continued to drop them into their pails. Even the Czech and Russian guards spent time sifting the earth and gathering the gems. Everyone dug, hoed, and uncovered the treasure. I still have a small piece of folded paper containing some of the grains of those garnets, but both Stariņ and Valdis boast of a much larger treasure trove. Though the deposits are now generally considered depleted, some small mining operations still exist there in the vicinity of Podsedice.

Podsedice

Stariņ and Valdis with Anna in Podsedice

Maruta, Dagnija, and Stariņ in Podsedice

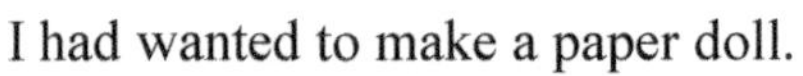

I had wanted to make a paper doll.

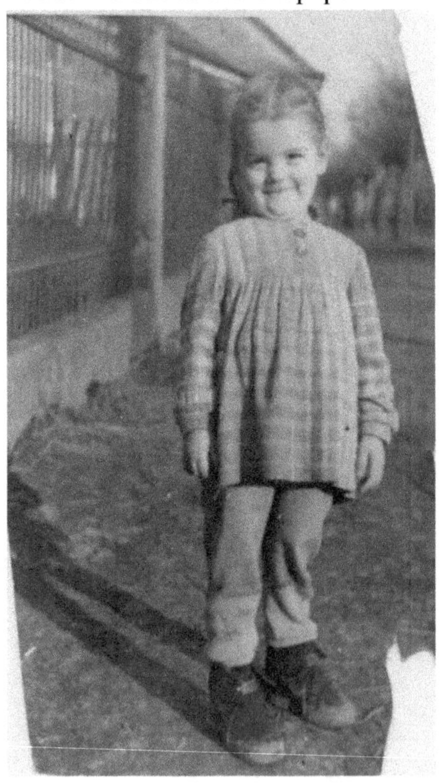

CHAPTER EIGHT

THE WAR'S END

In April, 1945, in his subterranean *Führerbunker* Adolf Hitler finally realized the futility of his campaign to make Nazi Germany the most powerful political force in the world. There, on April 30, as the battle for Berlin raged above, he and his Eva committed suicide. In a matter of days, Hitler's forces in Berlin capitulated, followed shortly by his other armies in Europe. On the morning of May 7, 1945, General Alfred Jodl of the German High Command signed terms of unconditional surrender on behalf of his government. Eisenhower's Chief of Staff Walter Bedell Smith and others signed for the Allies. After a ceremony in Berlin had ratified the terms, the war in Europe was finally declared to be over.

The following day, May 8, was celebrated as V-E Day, the day of victory in Europe.

On May 6 General Patton's Third Army liberated the major portions of Western Bohemia of the Sudetenland from the Germans. The rest of Czechoslovakia was freed by the Soviet Red Army. Patton's army remained in Czechoslovakia almost until the end of the year to help in rebuilding the area. His presence there made it possible for many refugees from the Baltics and elsewhere to escape capture and deportation by the Soviets. For our extended family this meant an invaluable reprieve.

Still, for the Baltic refugees, the end of the war in Europe brought no rejoicing. The struggle for the survival of their homelands had been lost. It meant that the Americans were halting their offensive, and now the Soviets would be taking over the territories. The Germans had lost, and nobody remained to fight the Russians.

Anniņa said that at one point, Tamāra was having second thoughts, and she thought that maybe the Russians had probably changed. It might not be so bad if we went back after all. It didn't take Anniņa very long to convince her that this would never be the case, and Tamāra sadly abandoned that fantasy.

SOVIET RED ARMY TROOPS entered Prague on May 9 in 1945. On the fifth of June, the Allies commenced dividing up the city of Berlin and the whole country of Germany, including its government. In Czecholsovakia all of the Sudetenland area gradually shifted to Soviet control. For our family and for all of the other Balts in that area, it meant that the unthinkable was again happening. Except for the temporary presence of General Patton's army, we were once more in Soviet hands.

Stariņ continues:

> At the end of the war in Europe in May 1945, in our area, the Czechs took over from the Germans without any shots being fired. One morning we saw white and red flags all over. The Czechs' flag is the same as the Polish flag. The blue triangle was added for the Slovaks, whose flag is white, blue and red, when Czechoslovakia was founded. Things were OK during the day, but at night Germans (the *SS*, it was said) used to come down from the nearby hills and shoot up the village. We were told by our mothers to lie down on the floor so that bullets coming through windows would not hit us, but I don't remember any window being broken in our house. The Czechs asked the Russians for help but soon were sorry. The Russian soldiers thought that the Czechs had been allied with the Germans.
>
> Because of the lack of more reliable news about our situation, our mothers turned to the occult. Anna's forte was cards. There was the time when a young Czech named Frantisek wanted to have his fortune told. Anna tried telling it from the cards three times and each time the "fortune" was death. I don't know what she finally told him, but later that same night he was stabbed by a Russian soldier and died.
>
> The main source of "news" was something like a Ouija board, a saucer or plate with letters written around its perimeter, which supposedly spun when somebody put her hands on it, and somehow it was possible to read the letters forming a message that came from a spirit they had

requested. Roosevelt, who had died not too long ago, was popular. Rita said Lida (Lidija) was by far the best at this. Rita asked the spirit once where she would be in ten years. The answer was Buffalo (she pronounced the "u" as in "put", the way a Latvian would). Rita was completely mystified as to what that could mean when she mentioned it to me in Germany. I only knew it was an animal. It was years later that I realized that we had been living in Syracuse ten years after this and that we did go to see Niagara Falls. It would be too weird if she had actually been in Buffalo ten years afterwards.

Many Latvian women were burned at the stake as witches in the old days, although it is said that wives often denounced as witches women who were too friendly with their husbands.

AT THE END OF THE WAR, German installations in the Sudetenland ceased to exist. Tētiņ's period of employment as stoker with the Germans also ended, in a manner of speaking. The Sudetenland now reverted back to being part of Czechoslovakia. Thus, from May 17 to May 31, 1945, Tētiņ was employed by the "Czech National Rail Company" as a "manual worker," but his duties had not drastically changed from those he had had as an employee of the German *Reich*.

There were constant reminders of the perilousness in our lives. One day as Tētiņ was returning from work, a Russian car stopped in front of him. Drunkenly, the Russians stepped out, waving their guns in the air and arguing about whose turn it was to shoot Tētiņ. Just then another Russian car arrived, and the driver shouted to the gunmen, calling them back to work and probably saving Tētiņ's life.

IT WAS ALREADY IN OCTOBER of 1938 that Nazi Germany had annexed the Sudetenland under the rationale that populations of ethnic Germans living there necessitated the expansion of the Fatherland. Now at war's end, as a result of the overwhelming hostility toward these occupying Germans, the Potsdam Conference of late July 1945 determined that the several million Germans there needed to be expelled. Only those who could prove their anti-Nazi affiliation were allowed to remain in Czechoslovakia.

Punishment by persecution at the war's end found new victims. The ethnic German population had been in the area for generations. For six long years the Czechs had submitted to Nazi tyranny. Now they exacted revenge wherever they could. Anyone heard speaking German was attacked and beaten. Whether old or young, sometimes even children, they were pulled from their homes and pummeled in the streets. Atrocities happened on both sides. Anniņa observed a pair of Czechs walking too closely behind some German soldiers. A Czech accidentally tripped up one of the Germans. Frightened, the Czech immediately apologized, but the German shot him anyway.

In Podsedice it was no different, and many Germans there were also killed. Anniņa told of one young German listening to a song on the radio, *"Und wieder geht ein schöner Tag zu Ende. Ich lege mein Herz in Deinen lieben Händed."* (Another beautiful day has come to an end. I entrust my heart to your loving hands). To him, the song seemed to tell of the war's end and Germany's loss. When the song ended, he sang it to himself mournfully like a dirge.

The mother of that same German was arrested by the Soviets and dragged into a nearby house and beaten. Later they brought the young man into the room and made him clean up the bloody mess. As he swabbed the floor, he heard his mother whimpering in a room nearby. It seemed like all of the woes of the past six years were being blamed on a handful of Germans, and retaliation exacted on these same unfortunates.

MAMMA HAD FROM THE start of our residence in Podsedice been confined in a sanatorium in Aussig. The sanatorium was not in the town center but rather at the top of a forested hill.

Wishing to visit her mother, Anniņa took the train to the city. Leaving the station, she was accosted by a drunken Russian in a military uniform who commanded her to get onto his bicycle. Anniņa tried to tell him in her broken Russian that her mother was ill, and she needed desperately to get to her. The Russian said he would take her there. Whatever his real intentions were, Anniņa could only speculate. The rider was reckless and mindless of cars traveling closely in both directions, and Anniņa feared for her life, if not at the soldier's hands, then surely in an accident caused by him. They stopped once, and the Russian allowed her to dismount as he briefly disappeared. Just then, a Czech approached her on his bicycle. He told her that he had followed them from the station, and if that Russian had threatened her in any way, he would have shot him dead.

IN ANTICIPATION OF THE END of the war and Nazi Germany's imminent surrender, Roosevelt had met with

Stalin and Churchill in Yalta in the Crimea at the start of February in 1945 to discuss what should be done upon the achievement of victory. It was there that they resolved to divide Germany into four zones: American, British, Russian and French. Unfortunately for us, Roosevelt also conceded that he would not protest if the Soviet Union were to annex the three Baltic States. Henceforth, the Yalta Conference has been regarded by many as Roosevelt's "Western Betrayal."

On March 31, 1945, the statesmen concluded the final version of their plans in a secret codicil to this agreement. As a result, over two million Soviet citizens were returned by the Western Allies in return for the same number of citizens of western countries.

In subsequent years our parents and other American Latvians exacted revenge in their own meager way. Because of Roosevelt, a Democratic president, never again would a single member of that political party get their vote.

IMMEDIATELY AFTER THE GERMAN capitulation, the Soviets commenced repatriating "their citizens." For us the Latvian refugees, the greatest dread, of course, was to fall into their hands. One morning at six o'clock, there was loud pounding on the door of our home. Soviet soldiers had come to rouse us out of our beds in the Podsedice DP camp.

Daucis remembers that day:

> There were several Latvian families in the village where the Soviet troops happened to catch up with those

> fleeing them. The ones who came into the apartment where all of our extended family was gathered seemed clean-cut and very young to my not quite six year old eyes. I did notice that our blind grandfather seemed to be unusually nervous.

We were told to dress immediately and go and wait in the street, as we were to be taken home. "Home" could only mean one thing – Siberia. The Russians were insistent and threatening, and there was no use at all in protesting, so we got up, dressed, and waited in the street. Anniņa had earlier obtained a little chubby doll for my third birthday on May 28. She gave the doll to me as we waited there in the street because Anniņa didn't know if we would all end up together, and she really wanted me to have it.

Anniņa recounted:

> And do you know what happened? The doll fell out of your hands and broke! Your Mimmīte was upset, but I was ecstatic and said that it was a sign of luck. Indeed, it was a good omen! You see it turned out that the Russians, whose priority it was to transport some Russian and Ukrainian women had gotten drunk and had driven their trucks into a ditch, wrecking them, and as a result could not deport us. Imagine the omen of the breaking doll!

Daucis summed it up, "We all owe our survival, and our children their very existence, to drunk driving!"

Anniņa often saw deeper meanings in day to day occurrences, and this particular day seemed to have been written in the stars. So again we persevered and could turn our attention once more to planning an escape.

THIS LAST EXPERIENCE SERVED for us as an urgent call to action. The Soviets were committed to deporting us, but it was our duty to evade their plans and continue to lead a life in freedom.

Rita was very intelligent and adept at organizing and planning, though Anniņa said that Rita was "bossy." Well, maybe so, but Rita's guidance and fortitude helped as all to survive. Authoritative and exacting, Rita was undoubtedly the dominant sibling of the Bištēviņš family. She had specialized in philology, the study of language, at the Rīga University, which helped us all in the current circumstances. Rita was the one who weighed the possibilities of whether we should stay in any one place, and when it would be time to move on. Now again, she took command of the situation and decided that we must undertake something rather than surrender to the circumstances.

The plan was for her and Anniņa to make their way to Prague, a journey of some 70 km. They would try to get to the American Embassy in an effort to find a way of immigrating to America. Rita's brother-in-law, the only person we knew in America, was a ship's captain in New York, and he would surely help in sponsoring our families. Unfortunately, as it turned out, Rita's brother-in-law Reinis Šnore died in 1948 before any further plans could materialize.

Arriving in Prague, Rita and Anniņa made their way to the American Embassy. However, all of their carefully laid plans had to be postponed, as Russian soldiers were now standing at the gates with rifles. When the soldiers finally left, the women approached the building and somehow were able to get inside. They remembered the plan they had used previously when trying desperately to get to another refugee camp the time when Marutiņa was so very sick. It might work again. They would claim to be German, maybe even one of those who had to be expelled from Czechoslovakia.

Stariņ related Rita's provisional plan:

> Incidentally, my mother (Rita) had looked into the possibility of "repatriation" to Germany. Her thinking had gone along these lines: I communicate with our Estonian relatives in German. This could be stretched to say that we speak German at home. She also had majored in Germanic languages at the university, her thesis being about some aspect of the ancient Gothic language. When she got to the Embassy or wherever this was handled, she was given a document to sign. It started, "*Ich bin Deutsch*" (I am German). Instead, she walked out.

BOTH RITA AND ANNIŅA HAPPENED to be in Aussig on July 31, 1945, and witnessed what is known as the Ústí Massacre. They had just visited Mamma at the sanatorium.

Making their way to the station in Aussig, they observed soldiers running wildly through the streets. Panicking, they sought sanctuary in a church to escape the chaos. There Anna absently ran her nails against something on the wall. Hearing the soft screech, a priest appeared and ordered them out.

"You can come in only to pray. There is no treasure here."

Anniņa pleaded, "I'm afraid."

"Out!" he shouted at them.

Leaving the church, they sought safety in a café. Presently bombs were exploding in the street, the earth was shaking, and everything around them collapsed into a heap. Cowering, they observed the surrounding chaos. Local Czechs ran screaming through the streets, attacking the Germans. The two women knew that the German presence had been deeply resented by the Czechs these many years, and they silently agreed not to speak for fear of being mistaken for one of the enemy.

The cause of the chaos was the explosion of an ammunition dump which killed almost thirty people including seven Czechs. The blame for it was placed on German saboteurs, leading immediately to a massacre of ethnic Germans, recognizable by the white armbands they wore. Any German seen in the area was beaten or stabbed with bayonets. One man who shouted a provocation was thrown into the Elbe River followed by several others, even a woman carrying a baby. There the floundering victims were shot by Czechs and Soviet soldiers. The number of people killed fell within a wide estimate, but later it was revealed that twenty-four bodies of these victims had been disposed of in the crematoria of the nearby Theresienstadt concentration camp.

To the Czechs, the massacre justified the expulsion of the ethnic Germans, which followed soon thereafter. In the end, some twelve million of them had fled or been ousted from the Sudetenland and other territories of Eastern Europe.

Stariņ has some more to say on the subject:

It must have been June or July that the Germans were expelled from the Sudetenland. The Germans had lost their privileges when the Austro-Hungarian Empire broke up, as they did in Latvia after WWI. As a result, they had supported Hitler's occupation of Czechoslovakia and were probably more Nazi-oriented than the Germans of Germany and definitely more so than the German soldiers recuperating occasionally at our relatives' farm in Latvia (Ziņģi). According to Rita, if one went to a German store and did not greet them with "Heil Hitler," they would not sell to you. In times of shortage the shopkeeper is king. Our mothers also had problems at Czech stores, because hearing them speak Latvian, the Czechs thought they were Hungarians, the other ruling nation in the old empire. Latvian may sound a bit like Hungarian because in both languages the first syllable is always stressed and both have a lot of "s" and "sh" sounds.

Back to the expulsion, I have a clear picture in my mind's eye of people putting small amounts of belongings on narrow flat-bottomed carts (looking like oxcarts with the sides removed). It was obvious that there was not enough room in the carts for the people, who'd have to walk. Czechs wearing khaki uniforms stood around them, holding what looked like large ping-pong paddles with the flat part replaced by a sheet of red rubber, most of it cut into narrow strips. I sometimes wonder what became of Annemarie and Rosemarie.

AFTER THE WAR, THE SOVIETS acquired control of Czechoslovakia, and the Allies divided Germany into zones just as the Yalta agreement had stipulated. Our goal was to somehow make our way to any area other than Soviet, preferably, of course, American. Another Latvian family in Podsedice, the Liepiņš, with whom we were friendly had also decided to flee and had formulated a plan for getting into the American zone. Shortly before setting out, they invited Anniņa for a walk, and in low whispering tones confided to her their intention. They would be leaving quite soon, and if and when they made it to the American zone successfully, they would contact us. For this we agreed on a coded method of communication whereby they would signal to us their success. Perhaps our group could then try a similar means of escape.

The Liepiņš family had already been gone for some time, when Anniņa received a post card with the message, "The operation was successful. The girl is doing well."

Now the challenge was up to us. Buoyed by the news that had arrived, we planned in earnest. Success was an absolute necessity, for if we failed, the Russians would take us back to Latvia in their big trucks and boxcar trains. Everything needed to be kept a secret, as anyone overhearing our plans could betray us.

Anniņa had a good friend, Mr. Zeman, a Czech, who was the village pharmacist. He was aware of the dangers and sympathized with our family's situation. As we would not be able to go anywhere without permission, he wrote us a document to be presented to the town authorities. This might provide us with safe passage out of town. He also gave Rita a supply of medications for Mamma for her asthma. Years later, Rita told her sons that Anniņa had also asked the pharmacist for poison for herself in case our group fell into Soviet hands. But Mr. Zeman looked at her sympathetically, and said, "You are much too beautiful for suicide."

We would need one of the flat-bottomed carts with the long pole handles for our journey. It would come in handy for the children and for Mamma, as it would enable a more speedy departure. Tētiņ offered cigarettes to a German woodworker to have such a wagon constructed for us. Unfortunately, we soon discovered that although he took our cigarettes, the woodworker failed to fulfill his part of the bargain, leaving us to our own devices. We would all have to be on foot.

To get to safety, it was necessary to cross the expanse of a bridge. Though she was being supported on both sides, it was difficult going for Mamma, who experienced a severe asthma attack. After Anniņa gave her some of the medicine from the Czech pharmacist, Mamma's attack subsided, and we were able to continue on and get to the other side.

At the nearest railroad station, we managed to board an already crowded train full of refugees desperate to stay ahead of the Soviet advance. Arriving at the next station, Soviets forced everyone off the train and commandeered it for their own use. Thus expelled, our group of twelve and the other passengers spent the night hiding in the forest waiting for yet another train to arrive. When it finally did come, it was so full that people even rode on the train's steps. Somehow, our grandparents managed to keep up with us. One blind, and the other asthmatic, they both still exhibited so much courage, keeping pace with us without ever complaining.

At one station, most of our group had already boarded a train, but Tētiņ was still on the platform. Two controllers, a Czech and a Russian, called several of the men including our father out of the line. Supposedly they were looking for conscripts or for other work that they wanted to have done. In

Russian, Tētiņ said to them, "I am Latvian," and after quite some time, they allowed him to join our family on the train. Perhaps they thought that he would serve them only temporarily, as he would surely soon be repatriated.

CHAPTER NINE

MARIÁNSKÉ LÁZNĚ,

August 1945

Some 79 miles to the southwest of Podsedice in an area surrounded by lush green mountains is the Czech spa Mariánské Lázně, better known by its German name, Marienbad. The vicinity is rich in some 40 mineral springs, from which the waters at one time were exported to thankful recipients, a million bottles per year. In peacetime, Marienbad was one of the most important spa centers in Europe. Now in 1945, the local population of ethnic Germans was being expelled, as also elsewhere in the Sudetenland, and refugees like us took up residence – however temporarily – in the famed noble houses.

I have a document of attestation written in Czech and issued by the City Hall in Podsedice. It states that we were unregistered from their police files and transferred from Podsedice to Mariánské Lázně on August 12, 1945. The document is for all of us in our group of twelve, "Šnore Margarita, Sveķis Anna, Bišteviņš Eduard, Bišteviņš Marta, Neumanis Lidia, Neumanis Alfred, Sveķis Tamāra, and 5 children." This might be the document which the pharmacist, Mr. Zeman, provided for us.

There are other documents, a sheet for each of us dated August 14, 1945, and written in English and Czech. These were issued in Mariánské Lázně itself and stated that the date of taking up residence in Czechoslovakia was November 11, 1944.

Our home in Mariánské Lázně was the "Garage Mercedes," a building which had once been a garage, but now was a two-story house converted into apartments for refugees. Several families lived in one apartment, and blankets were hung up on a rope and secured with clothes pegs to ensure a bit of privacy. Mamma and Papus were housed in another building nearby.

We did not stay in Mariánské Lázně very long, but had to continue on in an effort to find our way to the American zone. The stipulation of the Yalta agreement that the Allies return all refugees to their homelands was at the time unknown to us. However, from previous experiences we knew that we must never fall into Soviet hands. Simply their nearness added sufficient desperation to our efforts.

Our own group spent a night or two in the city of Plzeň (Pilsen), about 76 km. from Mariánské Lázně in a US camp for DPs which was about to close. It was already August. The

U.S. forces had withdrawn in July from their occupied areas in Germany and now were working to free up those in Czechoslovakia of which they had charge. Plzeň and its refugee camp was one of these. All of Czechoslovakia was to be shortly given over to their war ally, the Soviets.

Ludvigs Žagars tells of how his family had almost been surrendered to the Russians. They were passing through an area near Plzeň and Mariánské Lázně, when they encountered two U.S. army trucks. The Americans commanded the family to get in and told them that they were to be taken to a camp from which they would be sent to Russia. Arriving at the camp, the family had extraordinary luck in discovering a break in the surrounding fence through which they were able to make their escape.

The U.S. troops were often coaxed into dealing with refugees they encountered in the area in a manner designed to placate the Soviets rather than actually help them. Although the war in Europe had already ended in May, actions necessary to put an end to the conflicts were still not in place. American forces commenced their withdrawal from the Sudetenland almost immediately though at an intentionally slow pace. President Truman and General Eisenhower had already recognized the threat that the Soviet Army posed to Czechoslovakia's effort to establish a democracy. It was not until the end of December of that year that both the Soviet and U.S. forces were finally withdrawn.

CHAPTER TEN

TO THE AMERICAN ZONE

August 1945

We moved from one refugee camp to another, not knowing where we were heading. At one station there were soldiers in Russian uniforms. In the next we saw American. From camp to camp, we boarded one train, descended at one station, spent the night in a camp, and boarded another train to descend at yet another station.

Daucis:

Subterfuge is a normal part of survival in difficult times. In May of 1945, Czechs in general had not yet learned that the Commies would be no better than the Nazis had been. Thus our mothers said that now that the

> war was over we were going to go back home (that would have been Siberia). Of course their intent was to head west and not east. Once the train was in motion my intelligent brother proclaimed that it was going in the wrong direction. Children were seldom, if ever, informed of ruses.

At critical times such as when passing through a checkpoint, we children had our mouths stuffed with candy, probably due to Stariņ's overly astute remark. Thus preoccupied, there was less chance of our speaking out of turn and innocently giving out inappropriate information.

Mimmīte later told us how carefully we children had to be managed and comforted during our travels through devastated Latvia and the rapidly changing DP camps. The grownups had to find ways to soothe us when we were frightened. Maruta remembered all too well the feelings of dread and desolation in spite of our parents' and aunts' best efforts. Being just three years of age at this point, I mercifully do not have any memory of these, our most dangerous years.

One bright morning, exhausted, we all descended from the train at still another station. Here we would again wait for another train leading to heaven-knows-where. Stepping onto the platform, the adults were perplexed and stared in disbelief at the sight. Could it really be? Men in American army uniforms were standing there, and an American flag was fluttering in the breeze in the bright sunshine. It took some time before our disbelieving minds accepted what we were seeing. This was the American-occupied area! We had arrived!

Stariņ's story:

One day we got on a train and went to Marienbad. We stayed there overnight, I believe, and went the next day to Karlsbad (Karlovy Vary), where we definitely stayed overnight. I think we crossed over from the part of Czechoslovakia occupied by the Soviets to that occupied by the U.S. (Gen. Patton's troops) between Marienbad and Karlsbad. Documents on the train were checked at the boundary on alternating days by Soviets (who were said to check them thoroughly) and Americans, who just glanced at them. Our documents were the grown-ups' Latvian passports (from a country that had been occupied and abolished). It turned out that Americans were the ones checking our documents that day.

From Karlsbad we went to Pilsen (Plzeň in Czech) and saw on the street a truck with an American flag and were able to get on it. It was taking refugees who did not want to be left in Pilsen, which was to be given to the Soviets, to a camp from which they would be taken to the U.S. zone of Germany.

It really made me feel good and gave everybody a feeling of security to see the Stars and Stripes flying over the camp (another vivid picture in my mind's eye). Our crossing over from the Soviet-occupied to the US-occupied part of Czechoslovakia was possible only because Patton had driven the Germans back faster than anticipated, occupying a part of Czechoslovakia, all of which had been assigned to the Soviets.

Anniņa's story about this part of our journey seems a bit more complicated. Well, though we were now in the American zone, we still had to find a way of being able to stay there. We did not know what was necessary for the

Americans to sanction our entry, nor how stringent the rules were, nor how exclusionary the selection process. Another problem was that the adults looked exhausted, and the children were so very pale. Someone at the station came up to our parents and whispered that they should put lipstick on the children's cheeks. They needed to look happy and healthy, and rosy cheeks meant healthy children. If the Americans discovered that we were not well, it might be less complicated for them if they left us in the Russian zone – leave it to the Russians to nurse us back to health.

The borders were already closing and we heard whispers that the Americans had already stopped accepting any more refugees, and panic gripped our beings. After all that we had gone through, were we really to be sent back? Maybe we could persuade the authorities that we were just traveling from one U.S. camp to another. In other words, we had to lie.

Rita and Anniņa were called into an office for questioning. In desperation, Rita talked and scolded, and talked and complained some more. The American interviewer soon got very tired of this.

Finally, he said, "Another word from you and you're all going back."

At that, Rita became silent and then humbly apologized. Now it was Anniņa's turn. Frustrated and on the point of tears, she told the American how desperate our situation was, how we had fled, and how difficult the journey had been for all of us. She lied and told the Americans that we had relatives living in Germany, that we had already been living in the American zone and needed to get back! This would be much more believable than telling the man that we had just come from the Russian sector. If they discovered that we were refugees, we could have been sent back, which had already happened to others.

Anna tried again, "We didn't know our way around and got lost. We do not understand anything that is going on."

"You're lying," he said.

"No!" Anna pleaded.

"You're lying!" he insisted.

For a whole hour it seemed, the official questioned Anna. Finally, he could stand it no longer.

"Look here, I know that you are lying, but I will let you stay."

He demanded our documents, and Anna and Rita showed them the Latvian passports. These the American did not understand. He threw them back onto the table in frustration and let us all pass through. And that is how we all arrived in the American zone.

Later telling me her story, Anniņa lamented that it's a shame that we were not able to again meet that family who had helped our escape by confiding to us their plans.

"I have never been able to thank them," she said. "They have no way of knowing that we all got out and into the American zone. But maybe somehow they did find out, as now and again, our names have appeared in Latvian newspapers. "

Ausländer: Lette.

Deutsche Reichsbahn

Dienstausweis Nr 347.

Gültig für zwei Jahre

Der in nebenstehendem Lichtbild dargestellte Herr Neimanis Alfreds

(Vor- und Zuname)

steht als Arbeiter im Lokheizerdienst

(Dienstbezeichnung)

im Dienste der Deutschen Reichsbahn.

Das Lichtbild ist von dem Inhaber eigenhändig unterschrieben.

(Unterschrift des Inhabers)

Lobositz den 10.1.1945.

Bahnbetriebswerk

(Dienststempel)

(Dienststelle, Unterschrift und Dienstbezeichnung)

05316 Dienstausweis für Bediens... A 6 q Steifpapier ... Wien VIII. 43 175.000 St. Q 0936

Tētiņ's ID when he worked for the
Deutsche Reichsbahn in Lobositz, Czechoslovakia

PASS
Permanant

TEAM 133 UNRRA

Name Neimanis Alfreds

born 18. 9. 1907.

at Valmiera

Nationality Latvian

Pass for

Profession postmaster

Hair

Date 20. 8. 1945

Eyes

Face

Height

Right Left

№ 009126

Tētiņ's ID card while in the Amberg DP Camp

CHAPTER ELEVEN

AMBERG

August 1945 to October 1945

Besides the division and occupation of Germany as decided at Yalta and Potsdam, plans were also put into effect to demilitarize and de-Nazify Germany, including its rebirth as a democratic society with efforts to rescue her economy. The British and Americans proceeded along these guidelines. The Soviets, on the other hand, immediately started establishing a German Socialist society in their zone which they patterned on their own.

At the end of the war, the Allies – U.S., Britain, and France established hundreds of DP Camps in their zones. Refugee camps even appeared in Austria and Italy. However, due to their ideology, the Soviets never set up any in their zone. Their idea was that displaced persons were expected to be quickly repatriated or integrated into their Soviet society.

Our first camp in the American Zone was in Amberg in Bavaria, just 65 km. from the Czech border into Germany. Finally we felt that we all could breathe freely and reveled in our new freedom. Now we were far from, though still so very close to, Soviet hands.

From August to October, 1945, our residence was in barracks in the Augsburg DP camp, that is, for everyone except Mamma. Upon our arrival in Amberg, she was admitted to the sanatorium and it was there that she stayed for the rest of her life. She had suffered from asthma for a very long time, and it was now further complicated by tuberculosis. The last years of her life had been a progression from one hospital or sanatorium to another, but she never complained or asked for anything, accepting her situation such as it was.

Our family was registered in the *Aufbauschule* camp and Mimmīte and Tētiņ were given little green identity cards issued by UNRRA, dated August 20, 1945. The cards did not have their pictures, only fingerprints. These would enable them to get food, clothing, footwear, and other necessities which had been donated by American churches in the U.S. Tētiņ said that they really did not need the cards, as everyone in the camp knew everyone else.

Tētiņ's sister Edīte, her husband Jānis, and Mammucītis were at that time already living in the DP camp in Lauingen. Edite was a doctor there, and her husband, who had worked in the Dairy Organization in Rīga, was the Lauingen camp's dairyman. In October 1945, he sent one of the large dairy trucks to Amberg to fetch us all and bring us also to Lauingen.

BY THE END OF 1945, the organization UNRRA had repatriated, that is – sent back to the countries of their origin – 5.6 million foreigners, among them 1379 Latvians. Still, that left 1.2 million, among them 160,000 Balts, who refused to return to their native lands, now run by Communists. The Supreme Headquarters Allied Expeditionary Force in October 1945 decided that Baltic nationals should not be repatriated by coercion. Still, they would not prohibit Soviet officers from visiting refugee camps to try to persuade the refugees there to return voluntarily to their homeland.

Reflecting on our escape, I must admit that we had really been very lucky. By mid-January, all of Czechoslovakia was under Soviet control. On January 19, 1946, all Latvian, Estonian, and Lithuanian refugees still remaining there received orders that they were obliged to return to their native countries to which the Soviet authorities shall deliver them. Having received this notice, several refugees still there immediately made a beeline in the direction of Czechoslovakia's border with Bavaria in Germany. I hope that they also were as fortunate as we had been.

To continue the task of refugee distribution, the United Nations decided on establishing a new organization, IRO. At this time also, a screening process was started to identify war criminals, collaborators, and other undesirable elements. Included in the screenings was the examination of the left arm in order to find out whether an applicant had one of those tell-tale blood group tattoos. This was to bring to light any members of the *Waffen-SS,* who generally had their blood group tattooed high up on the inner left arm. The tattoos were small, less than one cm. high and were useful in the event of a needed transfusion. If discovered, the presence of a tattoo was proof that the bearer had fought against the Western Allies. These individuals, therefore, had little hope of residing in DP camps or of emigrating. As a result of such screenings, more than a thousand DPs in the camps in Germany were expelled.

Circa 1940 postcards of Amberg and Lauingen

CHAPTER TWELVE

LAUINGEN

October 1945 to November 1946

The United Nations Relief and Rehabilitation Administration, UNRRA, had been in effect since 1943. It was intended to provide relief and sustenance to victims in areas liberated from the Axis powers after the war, but there was no offer of assistance to ethnic Germans. As a matter of fact, if necessary, many Germans were forced to vacate their homes and live with relatives or friends when their residences were commandeered for the use of refugees. Of course, the Germans resented this forcible eviction and watching their homes being converted into DP camps for the thousands of refugees. In anger, the locals adopted their own name for the DPs – *Deutsche Parasiten*. Later, in the 1950s, when their homes were no longer needed, as by then the camps were disbanded, they were refurbished and returned to the Germans.

One of the camps in the American Zone in Germany was in Lauingen in the district of Dillingen in Bavaria. The Ködel & Böhm Harvester Company had been founded in Lauingen in 1909 for the purpose of manufacturing farm machinery. Other Lauingen buildings housed a leather manufacturing plant. During WWII, the production of both was halted, and the German command forced the companies to manufacture Messerschmitt fighter plane body and machine parts and other combat equipment. Some 3500 slave laborers worked to make sure that Germany's forces would be well supplied. After the country's capitulation, the victorious U.S. forces converted these buildings into DP refugee quarters for displaced Latvians.

The leather plant owner's mansion became the DP camp school. This was the building of the beautiful stone staircase at the base of which rested, on a high pedestal, a Grecian urn. The staircase and a nearby overgrown arbor are often seen in DP photos of Lauingen, as these were the most picturesque places in the town.

The Sveķis family cousin now living in Esslingen, Edgar Anderson, looked into the history of the DP camps there and also in Lauingen and Haunstetten. As a favor to me, he made small trips to both towns because I wondered whether there was anything that I would still be able to recognize. Shortly after starting to take pictures of the buildings he identified from our 1940s photographs of Lauingen, a man came out from a nearby house and questioned him as to why he was taking pictures. The two struck up a conversation. Although the man had lived and worked on that street for 37 years, he had no knowledge of a DP camp, and, Edgar supposed, even much less of the forced labor installation. Still, at one time 3500 slave laborers from the concentration camp at Dachau worked and starved on this small spot. Edgar said that Lauingen's inhabitants now seem to be in complete denial as to the town's history. Indeed, they appear to have completely buried any knowledge of the span of the years 1930 through 1945. He said, "The irony is that people in other cities in western Germany have a similar mentality, and it is best to not even question anyone about that time. It makes them angry, even aggressive, and you won't be given a true answer anyway."

WE LIVED IN THE "LAUINGEN Latvian DP Center 94-288" in Lauingen near Dillingen on the Danube, Bavaria, from October 1945 to November 1946. The Messerschmitt airplane factory had been divided into individual rooms for that purpose. Our family had one room. Some of the DPs cooked meals for themselves, as communal kitchens were there if they chose to use them. There were no ovens for baking, but that did not matter. We ate in the mess hall where sugar and butter were served with our meals, and we were even able to bring some of it to our rooms.

The Lauingen American zone camp provided for its refugees very well. In contrast, the provisions for DPs in the British and French zones were somewhat meager. Since this was known by the refugees, during the spring of 1946, those able did their best to transfer from the British zone to the American one. As a result, by September the number of inhabitants in the American Zone had grown by 44,000.

Among the goods we received were American clothing, boots, and other footwear. All of these were used items, but so very welcome. CARE (Cooperative for Assistance and Relief Everywhere) packages containing canned food, chocolate, and cigarettes were sent from the American Red Cross. These gifts were wonderful, but Tētiņ said that by the time they arrived, the cigarettes were often moldy from the damp ocean air.

All in all, we were so well cared for that it was not necessary to search for food elsewhere, and anyhow, black marketing was illegal. The Americans were not at all kind to people who purchased things on the black market. When a woman was caught with a basket of eggs she had bartered from a farmer, the Americans tore it out of her hands and amused themselves by smashing the eggs against a wall. Items illegally purchased were always destroyed. At times, surplus products were even burned so that they would not eventually be acquired by black marketers.

We had enough to eat and lived very well. Often there was too much food. The Americans allowed us to keep pigs for pork and bacon, and we fed them our leftovers. Tētiņ's entrepreneurial brother-in-law, Jānis, arranged for local German butchers to make sausages for all of us. This turned out to not be a good idea, as some Latvians suspected that Jānis was making secret deals with the Germans. That, of course, was not the case. Jānis was always an extraordinarily honest and helpful person. From then on, he just had the pigs slaughtered, and the meat was divided up without its being made into sausages.

Tētiņ kept busy in the Lauingen camp with various duties. During 1946 he worked at four-month stretches at jobs such as property warehouse manager, food warehouse manager, and manager of the commercial department of the Lauingen DP camp. For each of these jobs, he received a Certificate of Work Completed. In his employment by the DP camp, as in his work as Postmaster of Džūkste, Tētiņ's work was always well ordered and meticulous, and he received praise from everyone.

A story comes to my mind now and then which Mimmīte told me. One of the camp women had a Negro baby from a liaison with an American soldier. This was a delightful little girl with a pink bow in her curly black hair. The time had come for the mother to emigrate, and for some reason, the authorities did not want the little baby to go too. A black American soldier had been sent to get the baby, and, Mimmīte feared, to dispose of her somehow. I told this story to Anniņa.

"No, they did not do that sort of thing," she said. "Several women had black babies with American soldiers. The women received presents of chocolates and other things, and then they slept with them. One saw these black babies here and there."

Anniņa said that Daucis had once told his mother Rita that he would like to have another brother.

"But a black one this time," he specified.

LAUINGEN WAS OUR FIRST camp with a distinctly Latvian community where we were free to exercise our cultural traditions. This alone seemed to lift everyone's spirits. At last, we all had kindred souls with whom we could share our experiences and lament similar circumstances regarding the flight from our homeland. Thus invigorated, Latvians developed their surroundings under the governance of the Americans. They were free to elect their own camp administrators. A school was established and volleyball and basketball fields were set up. A theater group and choir were formed. Scout and Girl Guide troops started wherever there were DP camps. Chauffeurs, having learned to drive in the Lauingen garages, ferried their fellow refugees to view the nearby Alps, towns, castles, and other wonderful sights in the big *Citroen,* which was made available for their use.

Initially, the Americans were somewhat apprehensive about schools being conducted in the refugees' native languages, but when they saw how adamant and how devoted to our national heritage we were, they soon relented. There was pride in this community in Lauingen. After the grueling and dangerous flight out of Latvia and through the Czech camps, it seemed as if we were on a carefree vacation. It was almost like being in our own "little Latvia."

DP CAMP INHABITANTS WERE thoroughly screened by the Americans. Two witnesses, which in these cases were our relatives, had to sign an affidavit that they had known both Mimmīte and Tētiņ during the time they had lived in Czechoslovakia from May 4, 1945, and in the U.S. zone of Germany starting from August 1945. The Americans needed confirmation that people who claimed to be refugees actually were.

Perhaps they also needed to know their backgrounds to determine if they possessed knowledge which could be important and useful to the Americans in the future. I suspect that it was for this reason that our parents were given an extensive questionnaire to fill out in Lauingen. I have no record of what was asked or what the authorities wanted to know, but Mimmīte and Tētiņ got receipts for having completed them. I learned much later that all along during the DP era, the Americans had known everything about each of us, probably with the help of the information thus gained.

ANNIŅA, AND RITA ALSO, were widows. Rita's husband, Austars Raimunds Šnore, died in 1941 at the age of 35, leaving Rita alone with their two sons, ages five and two. Rita noted in a DP questionnaire that Austars died of a "nerve stroke." Apparently he had to be hospitalized and was given medicine which turned out to be much too strong for him and he died. Anniņa said that the Communists had continually hounded and spied on him. He had been fired twice from his job at the Ķegums plant without reason. Throughout wartime, unending stories and whispers circulated. Some were designed to spare the innocent from further pain if it was at all avoidable. In our family, there were whispers that Austars had committed suicide. An exceptional student, he was a genius and had been employed as an engineer at the new Ķegums Hydroelectric Power Plant on the river Daugava. He had also authored several technical papers in the professional journal *Technika un Celtniecība* in 1940.

There was a time when Anniņa and Rita were forced out of the Lauingen camp. They were sent to Mannheim, some 250 km. northwest of Lauingen. Stariņ said that they were kicked out of the DP system because they were suspected of having entered US-occupied territory too late, a reasoning which did not really make sense, since we all had been together, and nobody else had this same problem. At any rate, what Anniņa told was a completely different story. The leader of the camp, a Latvian, called the two widows into his office.

"We don't want women such as you here," he said. "You probably never even had husbands."

This brought Rita to her feet.

"Mr. Bērziņ, do you realize what you are saying?" she asked. "You are ignoring what the fate of your own wife might become."

Indeed, exactly two weeks later he himself suddenly died, and his wife was left alone with their children.

Banished from the DP camps, they lived for some time in Mannheim-Rheinau. Anniņa said that they could walk across a bridge there and get very good German wine. In Mannheim she worked in an office, and Tamāra was employed to do kitchen work. Rita was hired by some Americans where one of her jobs was to shovel coal into the furnace of the house. Rita and her boys, on the other hand, lived in an unheated room in the attic. To keep warm at night, they used all of their clothes to cover themselves, the three of them all in one bed.

After Mannheim, they regained their DP status and lived in a Latvian camp in Babenhausen. Some children there had found a few live grenades, and playing with them had their arms blown off. From Babenhausen, Rita's family was sent to Darmstadt, where they stayed for several months, then Neustadt near Marburg, again a stay of several months, to Ingolstadt for a few weeks, and finally ended up in Haunstetten, where by then our family also lived. Tamāra had a cousin in Mannheim, and decided to stay there.

MARUTIŅA, WHOSE STATE OF HEALTH after her recent crisis had not yet completely normalized, provided much concern for our parents. She needed fresh air, they concluded. In Mannheim, Anniņa lived not far from the mountains, and the air there must have been especially pure, so Maruta was sent to stay with Annina to be near her healthy environment. Maruta recalls:

> This was someplace with good air, perhaps in the mountains. At night, I'd creep to the stairway and listen to adult conversations: how to interpret letters coming from Latvia, the coded language one would need to use, and how to decipher innocuous-sounding comments from them, of who had been shot or tortured: nightmare-evoking eavesdropping. Also, there was a book about the travails of war in Latvia, with photographs of unearthed torture victims in Rīga prison yards, basement execution rooms, families looking over their exhumed dead, pictures of their tortured bodies, General Goppers with a prison tag around his neck. It's sad to think that no matter how a parent tries to protect a child, things happen.
>
> When in the mountains with Annie, she would feed me Underwood's Deviled Ham sandwiches. These were so disgusting that I could not choke them down. After whimpering about it, which did not work, I learned to take them uncomplainingly, climb the stairs to my room, and deposit them in my suitcase under the bed. When it was time to leave, I hid, while poor Annie, packing my things, discovered the deception. I heard her startled exclamation at the layer of molding green deviled ham sandwiches that covered the base of my suitcase.

I'd return from one of these trips, and then you and I would lie under UV lamps in a medical environment, having illness irradiated out of us.

Because of her paleness, she was pumped full of whatever iron-containing food was available, most notably prunes and other dried fruits. These Mimmīte made into a delicious sweet *ķīselis* (compote), thickened to a slurpy consistency with potato starch. I loved it, but not Maruta. Even recently she complained:

"I still gag at the thought of that gloppy dried-fruit compote."

There was a time, though, when they thought it was the liver. During that noninfectious time, my hospital roommate was a little girl whose mother had died. What an unimaginable sorrow! But she survived with some equanimity.

I do have a ghost story about that hospital stay. There was a window overlooked the tiny chapel from which coffins were wheeled out onto the cobblestones. The Gothic doors would open to admit visitors, and then again to allow the coffins to be carried away. One morning I awoke, and approaching the window, found tiny palm and finger prints on the outside of the window. Perhaps a baby's ghost had wanted to join me in my room.

Among others in my photo album, there are some pictures of both Maruta and me with shaved heads. Apparently we both had contracted ringworm, and shaving our heads was helpful in getting rid of it. We had used the same comb to fluff a kitty's soft fur and then also to comb our own long tresses.

In Lauingen: the 5 cousins with Rita, Alīse, Pulkvedis Silenieks, Mimmīte, and Tamāra

Eduards Bištēviņš with his descendants.

Five cousins in Lauingen.
Maruta and I had our heads shorn because of ringworm.

Our uncle Andrejs visited us in Lauingen.

CHAPTER THIRTEEN

HERMANIS

My uncle Hermanis Bištēviņš, the brother of Rita, Anniņa, and Mimmīte, was extremely intelligent. He had been a teacher before the war, and his main interests were mathematics and physics. Anniņa told of growing up and being teased by her smart older brother. Unable to solve a math problem, she pleaded for his help. Hermanis glanced at the problem.

"You can't solve that?" he chided her. "It's so easy! Now I'll give you a problem which you really won't be able to solve!"

Hermanis never seemed to take life easily, but challenged himself to excel in everything which he undertook, whether in sports such as mountain climbing and swimming or in hobbies such as photography and chess. A lifelong teetotaler, he also frowned on smoking.

When Latvia was illegally annexed by the Soviets in 1940, its military was annihilated and replaced by Russian troops in short order. Whenever Hermanis spoke of the Communist occupation of Latvia, he emphasized the necessity of extreme prudence, as one never knew who might be listening. Anyone could betray you, and spies and secret police seemed to be everywhere. In May 1940 Hermanis volunteered in the Jelgava Defense Regiment.

All three of the Baltic States had groups of national partisans, known as the *Meža Brāļi* (the Forest Brothers) who undertook to wage secret guerilla wars against the Soviet invaders during their two occupations, and even into the years following the war. The Forest Brothers consisted mainly of former legionnaires, Latvian deserters from both the Soviet and German armies, and any persons whose only possibility of protesting was as members of fraternities such as these. Some Forest Brothers fought clandestinely in their own villages, while others took up residence in forests in groups each numbering about thirty men.

These were not the kind of battles in which Hermanis wanted to participate. Instead, he chose to fight an organized war, which at that time he did not consider totally hopeless. As it was, the German troops were stretched thin in all of their battlefields, and the *Waffen-SS* needed to increase their numbers in order to free up German soldiers for front-line duty. To this end, they called on non-German volunteers to fight the Red Army. The call was answered from all over Europe, and the largest legion was from Latvia.

Many Latvians resisted the German occupation. If victorious, the Germans could once more become lords over their Baltic land as had happened previously during the 19th century. However, for Hermanis and other Latvians, joining the German forces was still the lesser of two evils. They volunteered for the *Waffen-SS*, hoping that they could help the Germans achieve victory over the Soviet occupiers. Once this goal was realized, they would then fight to free Latvia from the Germans. Who would have thought that when the Legion was formed in 1943, the Germans had practically already lost their war.

Hermanis joined the 19th *Waffen* Grenadier Division of the *SS* and was assigned to one of the German police battalions which were transferred to the Legion in 1943. Sent to German-occupied Czechoslovakia for a month or so to train to destroy tanks, he was wounded before any major battles broke out.

The 19th Division was incorporated into the 2 *SS* Latvian Brigade. This division was deployed to defend the west bank of the Volkhov River near Leningrad during the siege of the city until late 1943. In this engagement near the town of Volkhov, Hermanis was again wounded.

After recovering, he and his company were transferred to the area of Ostrow and Novorzhev, just east of the Latvia-Russia border, training and waiting for reinforcements which were to come at a later date. When the Russians launched their offensive in June 1944, the 19th Division held its lines against these attacks. However, the neighboring 15th *SS* Division collapsed, allowing an attack by the Soviets and forcing the retreat of the Latvian – German troops. On July 13, the division crossed the Velikaya River near Opochka, leaving behind their heavy equipment which fell into Soviet hands. Captured and taken to Opochka in Russia, Hermanis somehow avoided imprisonment and went on to participate in the battles of More.

The More battles in the region of Vidzeme in Latvia's northeast were some of the fiercest on Latvian soil during the war. By the autumn of 1944, the Red Army had already captured the southeastern section of Latvia and was forging northwest toward Rīga and the gulf in an attempt to split the German fortifications. It was in More that the Latvian Legion of the 19th succeeded in repelling the Soviet attempts to break through to the capital, thereby enabling other German battalions to descend into Latvia through its northern border with Estonia. Having obtained their objective, the 19th Division abandoned the More defense positions during the night of October 5, allowing the Red Army to occupy them.

From More, Hermanis's company was sent to defend the German controlled area in Kurzeme in the "Courland Cauldron" battles. There he again sustained injuries which necessitated his evacuation. This occurred with the second to last transport ship removing the wounded from Kurzeme. He and others of his unit were later registered as being in Czechoslovakia in the American zone on November 5, 1944. Hermanis, with the rank of corporal, was decorated with the Iron Cross, Second Class, on April 16, 1945.

THERE WERE RUMORS AND speculation as to what would happen to the legionnaires following the war – would they be prosecuted as former *SS* and thereby imprisoned? Or would they be treated differently than German POWs? At war's end, the German prisoners were incarcerated in American and other Allied power camps. There they were put to work repairing war-demolished infrastructure, and in some cases were even allowed to earn money which they could eventually take back to Germany.

Most Latvian soldiers were at first confined in British POW camps. Hermanis, one of some 7000 men, found himself in the Putlos POW camp in Schleswig-Holstein, which had once been a former army barracks. This camp was in the north, just two km. from the Baltic coast. Not surrounded by fencing, the camp made it easy for its inmates to leave and go to the nearest town to buy or trade for goods. Numerous prisoners deserted, taking advantage of the poor administration and lax surveillance by the British guards.

The Latvian journalist, Uldis Siliņš, a former refugee in the Alt Garge DP Camp in the British Zone, told the following story. On August 31, 1945, the Putlos camp was visited by the Latvian choir from the Alt Garge camp. Following the concert, while the camp guards were distracted by two comely hairdressers, a handful of Latvian soldiers found their way into the transport vehicles returning the choir to Alt Garge and hid there, lying flat on the floor. "Whether true or not," Uldis Siliņš explained, "the fact remains that the following day in the Alt Garge camp, there were some 20 more DPs than there had previously been."

IN THE FALL OF 1945, the prisoners of the Putlos and other Baltic camps were transferred to the British-run POW camp 2227 at Zedelghem in Belgium, where 16,386 Baltic soldiers, including Hermanis, were imprisoned,. The day after their arrival in Zedelghem, the legionnaires had to undergo a body inspection. Disrobed to the waist, they were instructed to raise their arms. The doctor seemed to be interested only in finding the infamous blood group tattoo. In one officers' barracks, it was observed that out of 60 men, two prisoners had had an obvious surgical removal performed on the left inner arm above the elbow, while no tattoos were discovered on any of the others.

Compared to the seeming liberty in the Putlos camp, Zedelghem was without question a real prison. Surrounded by barbed wire, several sentry nests had been placed in the fencing, and these were guarded by young Belgian soldiers with automatic rifles. The guards, not yet properly trained, were often observed to be dozing.

At the start, the prisoners were mistreated and received just slightly more than starvation rations. They, who had mustered so much strength fighting for the freedom of their homeland, lacked the energy to fight the humiliation they received within the barbed wires of Zedelghem. Local people, seeing the suffering of the soldiers, came and threw bread to them over the fence.

The Soviets wasted no time in feeding their propaganda to their fellow Allies and portrayed the Latvian legionnaires as fanatical war criminals. As a result, Allies looked upon the prisoners with mistrust and treated them as if they were the Nazi enemy. Enboldened, the Soviets insisted on the surrender of the legionnaires for repatriation to the Baltics. Throughout the imprisonment, the enticers remained an ever-present sight in Zedelghem and around the camp, trying to coerce the prisoners into returning to their "expansive homeland," and reminding them that the offer of "freedom" was still at hand. For those who fell for the ruse and went back, some received no less than seven years at hard labor, while from others, nothing more was heard again.

Already in Sweden, in response to Soviet demand, more than 100 Latvian soldiers who sought refuge there had been surrendered to the Soviets. Those were dark days for the legionnaires, who feared that they also might be deported to the Soviet Union.

Even during their confinement in Zedelghem, the soldiers celebrated Latvia's national holiday, the 27th anniversary of the freedom which no longer existed, on November 18, 1945. There they assembled under the banner they had once carried in the battle at Opochka, and Roberts Balodis' 50-voice choir, along with the whole company, sang *Dievs, Svētī Latviju.* Good wishes were conveyed to the Latvians by the consuls of both Lithuania and Estonia.

PULKVEDIS ARVIDS KRĪPENS was a commander of the *Waffen Grenadier Regiment of the SS-32*, under whose leadership Hermanis saw action in Opochka in June 1944. At war's end, Pulkvedis Krīpens was among the incarcerated of Zedelghem. On November 26, 1945, Soviet envoys arrived at the gates of the camp, and upon presentation of some documents, demanded the removal of Krīpens and the other Latvians. At this, Pulkvedis Krīpens met the Soviets at the gate of the barbed wire enclosure, and in protest of the planned prisoner seizure, thrust a dagger deep into his own chest. He thus demonstrated that death was much more preferable to Soviet imprisonment. His attempt at suicide resonated with the authorities, and as a result the soldiers were not surrendered to the Soviets. Furthermore, the British headquarters in Brussels had no knowledge of any documents demanding the surrender of Pulkvedis Krīpens. The ones presented had been falsified by the Soviets. They were eager to have Krīpens out of the way because he was able to influence the soldiers to not fall prey to the Soviet enticements. Even as the Pulkvedis lay hospitalized recovering from his wound, the Soviets tried more than once to apprehend or "otherwise commit" him.

As the 1945 winter set in, the cold in the camp became unbearable. The thin barrack walls could not keep any of it out, and soon it was like the inside of a refrigerator. Condensation from the cold ceiling dripped onto the inmates, increasing their misery. Depression in the Zedelghem camp became extensive, especially when a group of some forty men relented and agreed to repatriation. They had lost the energy necessary to survive the cold and desolation around them.

The Latvian Red Cross in Germany sent a representative, Kārlis Gulbe, to Zedelghem to intervene on behalf of the prisoners and try to find out if anything could be done to alleviate their hopelessness and depression. This could perhaps be achieved by establishing contact with the outside world and determining if there was at all a foreseeable end to their current state of confinement.

Gulbe succeeded in mediating the exchange of letters from the prisoners to their families and loved ones in the DP camps in Germany. Even while he was still negotiating these terms in Belgium, the eager prisoners were writing and filling the satchels of the Red Cross representative with their letters. When Kārlis Gulbe left, he did so with his bags full of hundreds of them. These he forwarded to the recipients, even though the shipment had not yet been duly censored or screened.

Kārlis Gulbe had other good news to offer. Letters and packages would be allowed from the DP Camps in Germany. In addition, other Latvians living in Belgium were given permission to visit. As to their release, it was necessary to wait until the British would be able to address the subject, a prospect requiring more time.

Packages were soon being prepared by DPs in Germany. Though their own food portions were small, they nonetheless were able to put aside extras to be sent to their incarcerated soldiers in Zedelghem.

Bolstered by the good news of impending communication with the outside world, the prisoners' spirits rose. Within their own company, they organized instructions and readings, printed newspapers and journals, established choirs, and organized chess tournaments. During his yearlong detention in Zedelghem, Hermanis instructed his fellow POWs in algebra and geometry. At his release he was awarded a certificate in recognition of his "eagerness and readiness in improving his fellow soldiers' lives in their most dreary of times, maintaining an active life and hopes for better days in many hundred Latvian men's hearts."

One of his fellow POWs in Zedelghem was Roberts Balodis, a Jelgava acquaintance of our companion refugee, Tamāra Sveķis. After finishing his education in the Jelgava Teacher's Institute, Roberts worked as a teacher and conductor of the choir *"Dziedonis"* (Melodist) in Jelgava. In Zedelghem he founded another choir made up of more than 50 voices and named it again *"Dziedonis."* After the liberation of the Zedelghem prisoners, the choir remained intact and presented no less than 100 concerts in Germany, the first of which took place on the Latvian national holiday, November 18, 1946. It ultimately disbanded, as one after another of the singers joined the waves of emigration to lead new lives in newly adopted countries. Thanks to Hermanis, Roberts was reunited with Tamāra after being discharged from the camp, and they were married in 1949 in Schwäbisch Gmünd in Germany, where Roberts was a DP camp police officer. After their immigration to the United States and to the city of Long Island, the choir *"Dziedonis"* was reborn with new members among the many Latvians living there.

The incarcerated soldiers took an interest in sports activities about which they read or to which they listened on the radio. Taking part in sports themselves was not possible as due to their poor nourishment, their health status and lack of strength would not allow it. They managed instead to construct works of art from pieces of discarded materials they found – empty food cans, cardboard boxes, pieces of wood, and the like.

The most important act of the legionnaires in Zedelghem was the establishment, in December 1945, of a self-help organization to provide support for themselves and their families. Named *Daugavas Vanagi*, the "Falcons of Daugava," it was at the time the largest combat self-help organization. Because of it, soldiers were able to establish communication among the DP camps in Germany. The association operates uninterrupted to this day in the countries to which DPs have emigrated. Still, the Soviets continued to denounce it as a Nazi front, charges which the Russians echo even to the present day.

WHILE STILL INCARCERATED, the legionnaires could once more turn their attention to the search for their loved ones. For a long time, nobody in our refugee group knew of the whereabouts of Hermanis, or even whether he was alive. He tried in various ways to send requests for information of his parents and siblings. I suspect that an ad which appeared in the November 2, 1944, issue of the Latvian newspaper *Tēvija* was placed in his behalf by a Fr. Romanis, since the date was quite late during our flight. It listed our family by name, "Alfridu, Lidiju, Marutu and Dagniju Neimaņus of Džūkste." The ad and its date could well coincide with his evacuation with other wounded soldiers, since he was registered as being in Czechoslovakia from November 5.

Hermanis finally had success with a request dated November 20, 1945, which was sent on a Prisoner of War post card addressed to the UNRRA Latvian refugee camp in Amberg. Possibly he had heard that our group's last known address had been in Podsedice. In that case, Amberg, in the US Zone, would be a logical next destination for us. The authorities in Amberg conveyed the card to Rita, who immediately sent an answer, "Have received your card. Everyone is well. Come as soon as possible. Waiting for you." This, apparently, did not reach her brother soon enough, because on December 16, he sent another request. His return address this time was the Latvian Red Cross in Brussels, Belgium.

It was not until the spring of 1946 that the release of the legionnaires came about. The Allies finally realized that the Latvians were not Nazis despite the *SS* uniforms which they wore. Even at their liberation, the Bolsheviks did not let the opportunity pass by, but once more sent their envoys to convey to them the news personally that, if they wished, they would be welcomed to return to Latvia. They would be forgiven for their previous enlistment and would not be executed. Out of 13,000 soldiers, only 116 agreed to be repatriated, and these all had Russian names.

Hermanis was in the last group to receive its freedom. His official Certificate of Exemption states that he was "discharged from Disarmed German Forces on 21 May 1946 and is hereby exempted from persecution under the provisions of Article I of Military Government Ordinance No. 13 for the ensuing period of thirty days ending 20 June 1946 inclusive." The majority of the internees were transferred to various DP camps in the British zone, and others to England.

Having discovered the whereabouts of their relatives, the soldiers longed for a reunion with them. If that were not possible, at least the permission to live in a community with their countrymen would be better than nothing. Unfortunately, camp regulations did not allow it. Some ex-soldiers nevertheless disregarded the rules and succeeded in registering for the refugee camps without disclosing their former status.

When the war ended, the International Red Cross was prohibited from providing aid to German Prisoners of War inside Germany. By early 1946, the restrictions were still allowed, but only to a very small degree. Still, by August of 1946, twenty-three men in their company were not able to receive the aid that they all so desperately needed. To help these veterans, the editor of the Latvian newspaper, *"Latviešu Vēstnesis,"* donated 50 Marks to each of them for the purchase of food to last for two months. The very grateful veterans, one of them Hermanis, expressed their thanks in a letter published in the newspaper August 17, 1946.

Some legionnaires were found to be infected with tuberculosis and were treated in the local German hospital in Belgium. However, since they were officially classified as Germans, they did not receive medication or other support from UNRRA, and had to beg for help from the DPs.

BY MID-1947, MORE THAN TWO million German prisoners were situated in the American zone of Germany. It was up to the U.S. Army to guard these POWs. In addition, the army was also in need of guards to protect their military equipment, property, depots, as well as apartments, clubs, and shops for the staff, as these all were constantly being looted by German civilians.

In January 1947, the American military initiated a work program encompassing transport and guard duty to be carried out in several German cities. Latvians who stayed in Germany because they could not emigrate due to their refugee or legionnaire status found livelihoods and brotherhood in these programs, especially if they were young, strong, and capable of performing the job. Hermanis and many other former Latvian legionnaires joined the *Virsaiša Viestura Rota,* a company named for a 13th century Zemgale chieftain. This was the 8920th U.S. Army company in Stuttgart, Germany, composed of about 270 men.

The legionnaires had obtained their freedom from the POW camps only after painstaking security screenings made certain that they had not been involved in Nazi crimes during the war. Since all of them were former soldiers, they were familiar with the type of duties expected of them, and the only training they needed was to be familiarized with American regulations. They wore used American uniforms which had been dyed black, earning the wearers the designation *Melnie* (Blacks). Though officially the Latvian nation no longer existed in the eyes of many countries, the *Melnie* were able to stand at attention behind their red-white-red Latvian flag during inspections of their guards-of-honor formations.

Besides watching over military supplies and installations for the Americans, the *Melnie* served at the Nurnberg Tribunal from 1947 to 1949. The trial for the 23 major Nazi criminals had already taken place commencing in November 1945. Still to be tried were the actual expeditors of the Nazi crimes, which included the 177 doctors, jurists, *SS* and policing unions, the executors, and other officials. It was with these twelve trials that the *Virsaiša Viestura Rota* was involved. They not only guarded the prison cells, but the Baltic soldiers accompanied the prisoners to cross-examinations and also on their outdoor walks. Only two functions at the Nurnberg trials were carried out by the American military police themselves – accompanying the prisoners to the court proceedings and finally also to their hangings. The Americans found the Balts to be trustworthy and honest, and they were confident with the service which they received.

Hermanis told the following story about guard duty. Before the formation of the *Virsaiša Viestura Rota*, the Americans used Poles to watch the prisoners. When news came back to the Americans that the Poles were too brutal in their treatment, they substituted Balts in their stead.

Suspecting that their replacements were responsible for the loss of their jobs, the Poles, making use of the knowledge of the blood group tattoos, accused the Latvians of being *Waffen SS* members. This led to an inner left arm inspection which revealed nothing. Apparently the Germans had not been consistent enough in their job of tattooing, and many of the Baltic *Waffen SS* had been overlooked. Actually, if the Americans were really using the tattoo as a positive indication of Nazi *SS* recruits, this discovery in many instances would have happened much earlier during previous screenings. As it was, Hermanis and many others previously incarcerated in Zedelghem received a clean slate.

It should also be noted that being a member of a criminal organization does not in itself mean that one is a criminal. All over postwar Europe, the discovery of these left arm tattoos was sure to classify the bearers as the enemy. Soldiers transferred to DP camps were unable to hide anything. They were all registered, screened, searched, and interviewed before receiving permission to immigrate to any country.

Nevertheless, postwar soldiers crossing country frontiers were often subjected to inspections at military installations. If tattoos were discovered, no document excusing the fact would be honored. The blood group tattoos invariably led to prison and in many cases to forced labor.

HERMANIS HIMSELF OFTEN HAD many a tale to tell and laughed heartily at his own foolhardiness. The following happened during the latter years of his service in the *Melnie* company with the U.S. Army. Apparently, he suffered from narcolepsy, often falling asleep without warning, sometimes even while standing. Among his duties was to guard one of the facilities in the middle of the night. He had trouble staying awake, and this worried him, since getting caught napping could mean a serious punishment. During the night, other guards came to inspect those on duty. Hermanis took careful note of the time the inspections took place and got a brilliant idea. He had a small alarm clock which he set to a few minutes before the inspectors would arrive and hid it under his cap. The alarm would go off, waking him, and he was ready and standing at attention by the time the inspectors arrived. As this happened to work very well, he told the story to his comrades at arms, who could not resist playing a trick. Unknown to him, they set his alarm clock to go off at a time when he and the guard company were all at attention, presenting arms to the commander. There they all were, standing straight and tall, as Hermanis' alarm went off, loud and clear.

HERMANIS EARNED SOME MONEY working as a photographer in an American officer's social club for which he was paid quite well. He set up a darkroom laboratory and printed the photos himself. These were very appreciated by the Americans, though they soon realized that they could save money by doing their own photography. Subsequently, Hermanis was hired as a photographer in an American Negro Officers Club.

IN 1950 DURING EFFORTS TO resettle former soldiers and refugees, Hermanis had agreed to be sent to Australia, though circumstances made him remain in Germany. Stariņ said that Hermanis' chest x-ray showed that he had tuberculosis in his lungs, and he was thus screened out from immigrating to America, and possibly also to Australia.

Years later, when restrictions were eased, his sisters did their best to encourage their brother to join them in the U.S.A., but Hermanis never did, deciding instead to live his life in Germany. Already in 1946, Latvians remaining there founded a Latvian *Ģimnāzija* (high school) in Detmold. In 1957, the school moved to Münster in Nordrhein-Westfalen, where he served as a professor of science and mathematics, and where he lived for the rest of his life.

GRADUALLY, THE LAUINGEN CAMP was liquidated, and by November 1946, all of its DPs were moved to either Kleinkötz near Günzburg on the Danube, or to the Augsburg DP camps Haunstetten and Hochfeld, which were much larger and therefore more economical to operate. UNRRA arranged for our group's transfer to Haunstetten, some 70 km. from Lauingen.

Edīte and Jānis Platais' family was assigned to the DP Camp Kleinkötz, just 30 km. from Lauingen. There Edīte worked as the camp doctor and Jānis served as the secretary of *AUSMAS*, a division of the camp government. The Platais' new son, Jānis Egons, was born in September that year. Little Jānis was Edīte's second child. Her first baby, Jurītis, had been born in April 1945 and died one month later of a stomach infection contracted after his birth while still in the hospital. It was also in Kleinkötz that Edīte's third baby, a girl, Ieva Ruta, was born on November 11, 1948.

UPON THE CLOSING OF THE CAMPS and at the start of the emigrations, new problems arose. As former legionnaires, it was still not possible to immigrate to the United States. Some families decided to break up, even divorcing officially, so that the wife and children could resettle. The husband would search for some other means to rejoin his family at a later time. Immigrations to the United States commenced in 1948, but it was not until 1951 that former legionnaires were permitted by law to follow. Nevertheless, even before 1951, some former soldiers managed to accompany their families by not mentioning their wartime status. To enable the families to not be separated, several emigration commissioners turned a blind eye, and sometimes even encouraged the applicants to make no mention of their past lives.

TOWARD THE END OF 1946, yet another campaign was launched by UNRRA to try to persuade the refugees to return home. The Soviet regime of Latvia participated in this with propaganda brochures and appeals. In some cases, it attempted to convince refugees to return by using false patriotic and anti-communist letters composed by the employees of the USSR special services.

Hermanis at enlistment

Right: his Latvian Legionnaire insignia.
Papus had it in his pocket when he died.

Hermanis and other enlisted men
In the 19th *Waffen* Grenadier Division

Hermanis in the service of the U.S. Army,
photographed with the seal of Latvia.

The *Virsaiša Viestura Rota* in Stuttgart

Hermanis as photographer

Dozing in his photo laboratory

1.Latv.divizijas Aprūpības daļa,Izglīt.nodaļa

Skola-Kursi.
1946.g. ..februārī. Apliecinājums.
Zedelghemā.Beļģijā.

Ar parakstu apliecinam,ka stl-mdk. ....
Bištēviņš Hermanis dzim. 1911.g.10.XI. Pernavā
ir darbojies latviešu karavīru "Skola - Kursi" organizētā mācību darbā par algebras
un geometrijas.......... lektoru laikā no 1945.g. 24.septembra. lidz 1.februārim 1946.g.,uzrādot teicāmu priekšzīmi,darba gribu un sekmes karavīru dzīves visdrūmākā laikā tādi celot darba rosmi un ticību labākām dienām daudzu simtu latv.vīru sirdīs.

1.Latv.diviz.štāba pr-ks.
maj.:
Aprūpības daļas priekšn.
kapt.:
Izglītības nod.vadit.
kapt.:
Skola-Kursi vad.
v.v.
Ģimn.skolot.

Attestation Hermanis received for teaching his fellow POW's algebra and geometry in the Zedelghem POW Camp, February 1946.

CHAPTER FOURTEEN

HAUNSTETTEN

November 1946 until January 11, 1950

In the early 20th century, the town Haunstetten near Augsburg in Bavaria had been just a quaint village in an agricultural setting. The Haunstetten block houses and other buildings with which we are so familiar were built in the early 1930s to house laborers, researchers, and engineers who came from all over Germany to work for the Messerschmitt company. This increased the town's population almost three-fold between 1933 and 1945. Preparations for WWII started there in 1932 in what is now the University Quarter. With its massive development of fighter planes, Haunstetten had become a wartime production center. The workers at that time already numbered some 18,000, of which half were foreign or forced laborers living in the nearby wooden barracks.

The Messerschmitt facilities and other buildings had previously been bombed by the American and British forces. For Haunstetten the war had already been over on April 28 in 1945, as the Americans then claimed that area.

It was at about that time that they came to realize the number of war refugees with which they would be faced. The U.S. military commandeered the block houses and the forced laborer barracks and assigned them for use as a refugee camp. It was in these block houses that our DP community found a home. The barracks, which had housed the forced laborers, were converted into our school buildings, workshops and offices.

In 1946 we were among only 500 Latvians in Haunstetten, but no doubt the number increased quickly and steadily soon thereafter. At the time, Lübeck with 6000, and Esslingen with 5800, had the greatest number of Latvian DPs in Germany.

Nothing in life was a certainty. We all had left Latvia, and since then we all were refugees. It remained up to each of us to make the best of whatever we could in this situation. No one could foresee how long we would be living in Haunstetten nor what we would be doing afterward.

OUR LIVING QUARTERS WERE in a room of an apartment on the second floor of the two-story housing block on Flachsstrasse, our entrance being number 60. The kitchen was shared with another family which had an adjoining room on the same floor, and our two families assigned ourselves adequate and separate times during which we would cook and eat our meals. Papus' bed was in the corner of the kitchen near the door to our room, and he remained there silently reading his Braille books even while the other family dined. I don't know who our neighbors were, but once the woman of the family saw me watching her intently as she sliced potatoes. "If you eat green potatoes," she said, "you will die!" – a warning which I never quite forgot, unconvincing though it was, even at that age when I still happened to believe a lot of what I heard. If Maruta and I happened to while too long in the kitchen, the woman would scowl, and Mimmīte, seeing this, shooed us into our own family room so that our neighbors would have their privacy.

Our parents and Maruta and I slept in the room which adjoined the kitchen. Tetin had obtained some wooden boards from which he fashioned beds for Maruta and myself. The mattress was a bed sheet stuffed with sweet-smelling straw, parts of which poked out at me if I moved around too much at night trying to get comfortable, so I learned to be satisfied with my sleeping position rather quickly. At that time I still had an occasional bed-wetting incident. One of these occurred shortly after Tētiņ had brought me some fresh straw. Without a word of admonition, he set to work replacing it. I saw the pained and weary look on his face. Not an angry word was uttered from his lips, but seeing him thus made me realize his sadness and disappointment, and it was the last time that I ever had such an accident. Words were sometimes not necessary.

A bathroom with a toilet and a tub could be reached from the hallway. This was to be shared with the other family. Nonetheless, Tētiņ and Mimmīte did not allow Maruta and me to use it, as they were very afraid of our getting an infection of some sort, so we had to do our business in cans, and Tētiņ went and emptied them in the toilet. This was especially a problem if we had a visitor, and we either had to hold it in or abandon any sense of dignity or self-consciousness.

We bathed once a week, when Mimmite took us along to the communal showers. These were reserved for ladies and children on Saturday evenings, and I found it very refreshing.

"Warm and steamy, and all the ladies naked and we too, and a cozy dim-lit golden time of comfortable socializing," was how Maruta remembered it.

USING THE GOOGLE MAPS website, I have been able to find the same Haunstetten block houses, and even to identify the building where we lived. Comparing old photographs with new ones, it is easy to see that some of the same objects are still visible in both sets of photos, from the block house chimneys to other landmarks, such as low curving walls along sidewalks in the area. The spindly trees in the old photo now show up as lush green blobs in the aerial views. Even solar panels have appeared recently on the roof of our old block house.

After his visit to Lauingen, Edgar Anderson also visited Haunstetten so I could see what the buildings look like now. In one picture he is standing at the very entrance to Flachsstrasse 60. The block houses were also home to Estonian and Lithuanian DPs, and at one junction of the camp, the countries' three flags were displayed in unity of our plight and in consolidation of our efforts to regain our national identities. Now and then the DPs from the three Baltic States would gather and march together through the streets of Augsburg with their countries' flags in protest against the illegal occupation by the Soviets. These protests were coordinated to take place on the same day as those in other DP camps in the American zone. We had no illusion that our demonstrations would bring any results, but marching all together would at least leave a bigger impression with the world's populace. We also did not dare to abandon our hope that once again our homeland would indeed be free. At such events all of the Scout and Girl Guide troops took part, and they were the ones entrusted with carrying the flags. At other times, these young people took over other voluntary duties such as postal delivery to the camp residents. With the arrival of new refugee DPs, the Scouts were there to welcome them and to help them move into their quarters.

Cultural life did not suffer in any of the camps, and theatrical and musical events took place often. Every camp seemed to be able to gather together a group of thespians to put on well-known Latvian plays for the entertainment of everyone. Latvian children had their own school in the wooden barracks nearby, and I assume that the Lithuanians and Estonians had similar ones. We thrived in our native language, as there was no need to learn German, or even to go outside of the camp grounds.

Many of us had national costumes, some made in the camps, and a few others had been taken along during the flight from Latvia. For various celebrations such as *Vasaras Svētki* and *Jāņi*, the midsummer festival, we children paraded with flowers in our hands and paper garlands in our hair. Maruta's and my national costumes were made by Biruta

Braslis, a fellow DP, and Mimmīte herself lovingly hand-stitched the decorative Latvian design on my vest.

Though my parents did not have a camera at the time, we still somehow collected enough pictures for our photo album. Refugees who had cameras took photographs of their own children and the local goings on and made the photos available to other DPs for ordering. Whenever new pictures were shown, Mimmīte and Tētiņ scanned through these, looking for the slightest glimpse of one of us and purchased any picture on which they detected a view of one of their two daughters. We did not need to be in full facial pose, but they recognized us nonetheless. On one is the sight of Maruta's eyes and forehead peering up from the bottom border of a school picture of a little boy's birthday celebration. On another is a side view of her strolling by in the background of a group photo of the camp's schoolteachers.

Due to shortages of food staples and medicine caused by the war, illnesses could become widespread due to decreased resistance caused by these deficiencies. The best way to avoid disease was prevention. It was not easy to keep the thin war-weary young ones healthy. Any illness that could not be remedied by Mimmīte's cure-all medicine of honey and butter mixed into a glass of hot milk needed something much more potent. One thing that did seem to be at hand was cod liver oil, which every family received for their children. In 1946 alone, Newfoundland fisheries exported six tons of cod liver oil and saved thousands of children from nutritional deficiencies. If our diet did not provide it, this was our daily supply of the vitamins A and D, ensuring our health by guarding against rickets and other diseases. Still, this wonderful stuff was the most vile-tasting medicine, and

Maruta and I blindly and obediently took our doses from Mimmīte's spoon following her command:

"Eyes closed, mouth open!"

FOR THE LONGEST TIME, EMIGRATION was not possible for whole families, as many sponsors seemed to prefer only single able-bodied men who were able to work well. My uncle Andrejs Neimanis eagerly accepted a job in the Canadian gold mines near Kirkland Lake in Ontario. There he earned about a dollar per hour shoveling rocks. With this money he was able to repay his sponsor for financing his transport to Canada. He eventually stayed there and took up residence in nearby Hamilton, Ontario.

One Christmas, I received a package from him which I eagerly opened. It was a Negro baby-doll. Cute, round, and of a smiley face, it was of composition material painted deep brown. Everyone laughed at my wonder at this unusual gift. Little did they know that the doll would become my dearest possession. Mimmīte, who had read Uncle Tom's Cabin, suggested that we name the doll Topsy, after the little slave girl who "never was born." Topsy only had one outfit, the one she came in. One of the camp infants, just a few months old, had become deathly sick and died soon thereafter. He had some lovely little hand-knitted clothes which the mother gave away after his passing. I very much wanted some of them for Topsy, but Mimmīte would not allow it. Who knew what kind of illness had led to the baby's death.

Before Topsy, I had another doll made of very thin unbreakable plastic, Rutiņa, and Maruta had her Birucītis, a rag doll with long rabbit ears. When we later emigrated to the

United States, it was to what was still the "deep South." The sight of little Topsy did not meet with approval from our sponsors, who drew Mimmīte aside and tried to convince her that a little white girl should not be playing with a "colored" baby-doll. To this, Mimmīte thankfully turned a deaf ear.

Maruta's poor Birucītis did not fare so well. Of cloth construction, it seemed to absorb all of the dirt and smell with which it came into contact. Mimmīte went through extraordinary lengths trying to save Birucītis, but energetic washing and suspending it by its ears on a clothesline did not help. Birucītis never did completely dry again, but developed a smell even worse than previously, and in spite of Maruta's tears, Mimmīte had to throw poor Birucītis away.

WE DID NOT HAVE OTHER TOYS, and they were not missed. Maruta and I had our own world of paper dolls. One time, clambering around Tetin as he worked at his desk, we persuaded him to sketch paper dolls for us, pretty ladies for us to clothe.

"We want them naked, Tētiņ!" we insisted.

He, chuckling, sketched in pubic hair. This did not sit very well with Mimmīte at all.

Maruta herself was very good at drawing and helped me. She drew my doll, and we each sketched them so many clothes and such fabulously colorful dresses, each with their rectangular hooks at the shoulders to ensure that they would not fall off. I can't think of anything that could possibly have been better. This was our wonderful world of make-believe.

One day, Maruta came upon the most perfect mattress for her paper doll. She found some white cushiony things in the closet. They were just the right size. She took one and gave one to me for my own paper doll. When Mimmīte discovered what we were using, she scolded us soundly, and reclaimed the "mattresses." These were her sanitary pads, and we were forbidden to make use of them. They were expensive and hard to get, and possibly the sight would be embarrassing if a visitor were to see them. Later, Maruta disobeyed anyway, and I caught her slyly helping herself to another mattress. I protested and said that I would tell Mimmīte what she had done. Maruta's tears started to flow, and she begged me not to tell.

"My doll has a sick leg," she pleaded.

This seemed like such a tragic event that I relented. I was very sad for her and her sick paper doll.

IN THOSE DAYS, GIRLS DID NOT wear long pants. We wore skirts and dresses, and to keep warm, we all had long stockings. These were not one-piece tights as children now have, but stockings held up by garter belts. They were invariably of knitted wool, and Mimmīte busily made them for us, garnering her supply of yarn by unraveling various other knitted items she received which we could not use. Sometimes the wool was reused several times or traded to other knitters. Unfortunately, the stockings were of very rough scratchy wool, and both Maruta and I complained loudly that it made our legs itch.

"Kož," we cried in unison.

Translated, this means "bite", which to us perfectly described the stinging, itchy feeling of the rough fibers. Mimmīte soon tired of our complaining and forbade any further discussion. Protest or no, they still itched, so we resorted to complaining only to each other, Maruta and I making up a secret communication, just "k," as in "The stockings 'k.'" Of course, Tētiņ and Mimmīte got wise to this very quickly and just smiled a bit knowingly. Maruta adapted reasonably well to wearing them, but I protested loudly and with tears. The solution was to stuff cotton handkerchiefs down into the stockings to protect my delicate legs from the "k" of the woolen fibers. This was better than nothing, but during the day the handkerchiefs shifted back and forth and made my legs look lumpy and grotesque.

IRO, THE INTERNATIONAL REFUGEE Organization, replaced UNRRA on July 1, 1947, to manage and deal with the care of the refugees of WWII. Unlike its predecessor, IRO painstakingly examined the status and legitimacy of refugees and their claim for assistance. Special attention was paid to the applicant's previous history such as any association with Nazis during the war, and if discovered, they were not accepted into the IRO-run DP camps.

The enormous number of refugees was taking a toll on the cost budgeted for their care. Strapped for finances, IRO found it necessary to reduce food allowances. Getting supplemental food elsewhere, such as the black market, was forbidden and impossible. As a result, some 35% of the children in U.S. camps were found to be under normal weight. Those in the British zone camps were even more malnourished. There was a serious lack of sugar, butter, milk, egg powder, and fruit. The IRO even reduced the number of their employees in order to not have to pay their salaries and to keep expenses low. German children, at least, had food provided for them through Hoover Aid.

The situation in Austria was even worse. Refugees there had to exist on only 1550 calories per day during a 2-year period, while DPs in Germany received almost twice as much. DP commissioners requested at least 2400 calories per day for the refugees in Austria. An increase in tuberculosis had been noticed in those receiving insufficient nutrition. In Austria refugees were even required to pay for their own lodging. It was not surprising, then, that those who were able to do so tried to make their way to any German DP camp.

A CAMPAIGN WAS INITIATED by IRO to prepare refugees for a productive future. For this, all able-bodied DPs were required to learn an occupation which they could practice in whichever country they would immigrate to at the end. The DPs greeted this plan very favorably, as learning a trade gave them not only something to strive for, but kept them well occupied. This was especially important, since working for Germans was not allowed. Workshops sprang up in all DP camps. The men learned to work as electricians, bricklayers, car and truck repairmen, and some to even drive the vehicles. In addition, there were workshops for radio communication and newspaper printing.

Women worked in kitchens and perfected their sewing skills. The latter was especially useful since used clothing arriving from the United States did not always come in compatible sizes and had to be adjusted by the seamstresses. Workshops and studios started for woodworking, leather goods, shoemaking, photography, and office work.

In effect, the DP camps were really quite self-sustaining with a camp leader who communicated periodically with the American governors. Both Anniņa and Rita, now once more with us in Haunstetten, worked as teachers. Mimmīte helped out wherever she was needed. Tētiņ was the manager of the warehouse. Everyone worked at whatever they were able.

In 1948 Tētiņ took a three month long bricklayer's course, since if he became proficient at the trade, it could lead to a good job in America, a very well-paying job. Upon completion, he earned certificates in three languages: English, German, and Latvian. Throughout the DP years, certificates of all sorts were doled out, either for jobs completed, or as was often the case, for none. The IRO even kept track of times when DPs were not employed, and one of Tētiņ's certificates states that for three months, January through March in 1949, he did not have a job. He never knew which certificates would be important, so he carefully saved them all – folded in two and slipped into a yellow envelope where all of his important papers were kept. Mimmīte received a certificate for having worked as a nurse at the Red Cross, however short a time that had been.

Shortly before emigration, he was given three more "IRO Testing Certificates." These would let any prospective employer in the United States know for which jobs he would be best suited: Locomotive Stoker, Postmaster, and Wood Carver, all three of which had somehow figured in his past occupations. As it turned out, however, Tētiņ did not find work in any of these professions in the U.S.A., especially not as bricklayer. Though the DPs learned the bricklaying trade enthusiastically, the instruction of it did not end up serving them well, as bricklayers in America were all professionals who had already worked for years at their demanding jobs.

Both Tētiņ and Mimmīte resorted to manual labor in America. After some years at menial jobs, often during the night shift, Mimmīte taught herself touch typing and key punch. As a result, she was able to get a much better position in a bank, enabling her finally to dress nicely for work.

Refugees whose livelihoods depended on attaining a university degree such as doctor were also met with disappointment upon their arrival in America. In order to continue in their professions, they were required to pass stringent examinations, most of which required additional years of study. As this was rarely possible, many doctors were resigned to assuming roles such as orderlies and other occupations requiring less preparation. My aunt, Dr. Edīte Platais, settled on a career of Medical Technologist in Milwaukee and enjoyed it very much.

TETIN'S GREATEST PLEASURE was in mastering the art of intarsia. Some Latvians in the camp already knew how to do the wood inlay, and he learned this trade from them enthusiastically. A workshop for woodworkers was set up in one of Haunstetten's barracks where anyone could learn to make the intarsia plates or to chisel wooden sculptures.

Tētiņ became very good at it, and soon so proficient as to be able to make one intarsia plate per day. This was quite an accomplishment, considering the amount of work involved. At times he simply lacked subject and design ideas. He had known the artist Ansis Bērziņš, whose family had ties to Džūkste. In Germany, Bērziņš, also a refugee, was a resident of the nearby Hochfeld DP camp. Tētiņ contacted him and arranged a meeting in the Hochfeld station. There they both sat at a table across from each other, Tētiņ plying him with cigarettes, and Ansis Bērziņš drawing sketch after sketch, about three to four pictures for one pack of cigarettes. (Ansis Bērziņš later immigrated to Colorado, and his drawings were often seen in books and on Latvian calendars.)

Using these designs, Tētiņ fashioned the most beautiful wooden plates. I still have the sketches, original artworks by one of Latvia's best folk artists. Tētiņ had taken great care to preserve the original drawings by making pencil copies of them with transparent paper and using carbon paper to apply the design to the veneer. This was usually put onto a light colored wooden sheet representing the sky in the scene. Tētiņ's favorite veneer for this was from the Karelian Birch tree. These veneers he used sparingly, as they were not always available. Karelian Birch has a beautiful swirling pattern perfect for representing clouds in a summer sky.

Back home, Tētiņ would sit at a table by our window, taking advantage of the daylight. A watchmaker's loupe was held fast to his eye pinched between cheekbone and eyebrow. Using a small sharp knife, he cut through a part of the sky veneer in the shape of a tree limb or a girl's sleeve. The cut out area was replaced with the veneer from a different tree of contrasting shade and grain pattern.

He did not use various veneers for nuances in faces as some of his colleagues did, but rather one single plain flesh-colored veneer. He often asked Mimmīte to lightly pencil in some delicate facial features. Telling me about this, he chuckled. "There was a man, Auziņš by name, who used different veneer for the mouth and eyes and even the nose. The result was really frightening to look at!"

Once positioned, these little bits of wood were then kept in place by small slivers of paper coated with animal marrow glue. And so he continued until the whole picture was finished. Some intarsia plates could be made up of a hundred minute pieces of contrasting wood veneers. The completed image was then cut in a circular form and glued into the central depression of a turned wooden plate.

Drechselmeister Lange was the wood turner who fashioned the plates. Though most DPs traded cigarettes or other goods to Germans, *Herr* Lange was beyond reproach. No, he would not deal in black marketing and required Tētiņ to pay cash for the plates. The veneer itself Tētiņ obtained from woodworkers in the neighboring villages. These people, unlike the *Drechselmeister*, did not mind at all being paid in American cigarettes.

Gluing the finished intarsia into the depression in the plate was a job in itself and it necessitated an extra-strong massive metal press. Tētiņ contacted a German ironworker and gave him the specifications that he would need. When finished, the press was so heavy that he had to bore four 5-cm. holes in the top layer, which made it a bit lighter, though it still weighed all of 35 kilograms. Payment for it was gratefully accepted in cigarettes.

The gluing of the intarsia scene into the center of the plate was accomplished with the aid of the massive press. This process was allowed to continue overnight. The stronger, the better, was Tētiņ's motto. The heavier the press, the better it would hold things together.

I only have one photograph where the press can be seen. It is in the right foreground corner of the last photo taken on the day of an excursion to Munich. That day Maruta, Valdis, and I accompanied Anniņa and Mimmīte by train to the big city. Whatever the main purpose of the trip was, I have forgotten, but Anniņa did buy two helium balloons. Tying one balloon to the end of each of Maruta's braids, she provided much laughter to everyone except me. As the balloons gently lifted Maruta's braids into the air, I can be seen scowling, jealous of not being the center of attention. I was finally pacified when we got home and had both balloons tied to the top of my head like a giant hair ribbon. It is in this picture that Tētiņ's iron press is visible.

Even in the DP camp, Tētiņ had some very appreciative customers. One of these was the Lithuanian architect, Mr. Mulokas, for whom Tētiņ adapted the Latvian folk costumes to look more Lithuanian by adding aprons to the ladies' dresses. A Lithuanian cross was also included somewhere in the landscape. Mr. Mulokas sent the plates to the U.S. to friends and family members. As payment, Tētiņ received chocolate for the children, marmalade, and a lot of cigarettes. Turkish cigarettes were not very good, he said, but American cigarettes were valuable in trading for other goods. One package of American cigarettes could buy one pound of butter. American cigarettes could also be traded for a variety of other things and services. One package of cigarettes could buy a train ticket worth several hundred kilometers of travel. This proved to be practical for attending sporting events or song festivals hosted by other DP camps.

A magazine for DPs, *Ilustrētais Vārds* (Illustrated Word), was founded and printed by an enterprising Haunstetten DP,

Eduards Raudupe. It served as a welcome entertainment by providing news about various DP communities in Germany and also included news of more worldly matters. Pages were devoted to sports, fashion, literature, and even a page for the little ones. The price was 3 *Reich Marks* per issue prior to Germany's currency change to *Deutsche Marks*. One whole page in the April 1948 issue of *Ilustrētais Vārds* is devoted to the woodworkers of our Haunstetten camp. Tētiņ can be seen in one of the accompanying photographs wearing a suit and tie and working industriously on one of his many projects.

He continued his inlay hobby for the rest of his productive life and made the decorative wooden plates, most often utilizing the Ansis Bērziņš designs. These he proudly displayed and sold at various Latvian functions.

ANOTHER JOB THAT TĒTIŅ had in Haunstetten was as DP camp policeman. His partner on the beat was a man from Skrundas *pagasts* by the name of Ēversons. Their uniforms were their own dark suits, and they received white armbands and helmets stenciled with "DPP" to signify their status. Their only duty was to walk around the camp making their presence known and look out for any unruliness. Otherwise there was not much to do except keep an eye out for the occasional boy with a stone in his hand, looking for mischief and a window to shatter.

Maruta remembers one night when American soldiers, scouring the camp while looking for deserters, kicked open our apartment door. They shouted as they searched our room. Discovering Tētiņ's police helmet, they were convinced that Mimmīte was harboring the deserter and demanded to know where she had hidden him. It took some time for her to make them understand. The standoff was finally resolved when Tetin, on night duty at the camp police office, was summoned to explain.

The Haunstetten camp housed refugees from each of the three Baltic States, each refugee group occupying one of the three long block houses. Some resourceful Estonians recalled their skill at distillation and set to work making schnapps. Eventually, the whole camp smelled of the spirits, but everyone went about his business and ignored it, including Tētiņ and the other policemen. They, and even the Latvian camp administrator, Mr. Kažoks, purchased some bottles for themselves.

"It was really very good schnapps," Tētiņ explained.

WE WERE QUITE WELL PROVIDED for in the American Zone DP camps. Being hungry does not at all stay in my memory. Still, for our parents, memories of the intense hunger we had experienced in some camps remained with them forever, and the availability of food was never again taken for granted.

"It is a sin to throw bread away. It is the staple of God's bounty," Mimmīte always said.

Their one consideration was always for our welfare.

"As long as the children have enough," I sometimes heard them whisper

I don't remember too much of what we had to eat, but *rupjmaize,* the Latvian dark rye bread, was most probably a big part of it, though sometimes it had to be prepared with the usually available American corn flour when wheat or rye happened to be in short supply. Sometimes we did have white bread, and heaven for me was a slice with a little smear of butter and sliced garlic on top. If sugar was available, then just sugar on top of the buttered bread was a close second favorite.

Occasionally we received CARE packages from the U.S. They were always very welcome, but we were at times puzzled by the contents. Inside one of the CARE gifts was *Crisco,* the shortening often used in baking in the U.S. Shortening was frequently included in the packages probably because it was easy to ship and did not seem to go bad. The greasy white fat was unfamiliar to Latvians and we had no idea what to do with it. Though tasteless, it was still fat, and as such, Tētiņ reasoned, it was suitable for smearing onto bread. So that's what he did, and as he joylessly ate it, he thought about bacon fat which was definitely far superior, especially with the garlic slices on top.

On one rare occasion, Mimmīte succeeded in obtaining a goose somewhere. She examined the carcass. "It's too old," she complained audibly. Still, the wonderful aroma of it permeated the rooms and staircase of our DP building, and it provided enough goose fat for Tētiņ's bread slices for some time to come.

Though the DP camps were off limits to Germans, a few peddlers now and then visited the peripheries of the camp. One came to sell ice cream – a dollop of rich sweet stuff placed on a small square of parchment paper. Or a balloon vendor would sell those colorful balls, lighter than air. Sometimes the parents would let the children trade for these goodies with toothpaste or soap, as we always seemed to have a surplus of them.

A book printer in Fischbach in Germany printed a cook book for the ladies of the Latvian DP camps, *Latvian and Modern Kitchen*. Mimmīte used it to prepare our meals in Haunstetten, and continued using it in our life in America. Unfortunately, as with many of the books and newspapers available during the DP era, it was printed on cheap acid-containing paper. The pages soon yellowed badly, then darkened into brown, and with time the edges and corners finally flaked away.

ON ONE OF HIS RARE VISITS, my uncle Andrejs appeared with two whole smoked eels. Latvians are fond of this luxurious fatty delicacy and even more so of *nēģi*, lamprey marinated in black tea, which in the processing somehow turned to jelly. Smoked and fatty, eel and lamprey were delicious on *rupjmaize*. Somehow, Maruta and I got our hands on the eels and stood there, each holding one, gripping the long tender sticks as tightly as we could and refusing to let go. Everyone laughed, but we had expressed our delight in a way that convinced Andrejs how his visits and his gifts were appreciated.

I don't know in which camp Tētiņ's older sister, Marta, lived. At any rate, we saw her very rarely. Edīte and her family lived in the Kleinkötz camp, and we did not see much of her either, though her name appears on health certificates of the time as our attending physician. Marta and Mimmīte never did get along, and I think that Marta hated Mimmīte with a passion. I could feel the venom in her without understanding it. Marta's attitude toward our mother must have originated a long time ago. She sometimes visited in

Haunstetten and brought chocolate. Marta was a single woman, good looking, and a delightful conversationalist. Undoubtedly she received chocolates from her many admirers. Then on her visits she made a big production about giving it to us, Maruta and me. One time, however, she made sure that Tētiņ and I were alone with her on a walk and that Maruta was not with us.

"Maruta will not get any," she said. "She looks too much like Lidija."

Ignoring Tētiņ's protests, she then extended the brown delight toward me. Though I was startled at Marta's unkindness, my eager hand took it, and wordlessly I put the chocolate into my mouth and swallowed it down. We had chocolate so rarely and I could not pass it up. I felt so guilty that I didn't tell Maruta and Mimmīte about it, but Maruta has a similar story about Marta and chocolate:

> One day at camp, she called me over from where I was playing with some friends. She held out a Hershey's candy bar and told me I was to eat it right there and not to share it with any of the children. To me it tasted like cardboard, but could have been luscious if we could have shared.

Yes, chocolate was a rare treat, as were candies and that wonderful chewing gum, the delightful soft sweet mass which never really disappeared, though it slowly lost its sweetness and just got mellower. We never could get enough of chewing gum, and my friends discovered that it could easily be shared. I watched as they took turns chewing and passing it along to other waiting open mouths. Once I was very lucky to get a piece all to myself, and after chewing it late into the night, I stuck it to my bedpost and continued chewing the marvelous stuff throughout the next day.

Whether by being told or just by observing unsanitary practices, Maruta and I easily learned what was not proper. A kind lady once invited us to her home to try some canned plums. She was making something that would require them to be free of the canning juice. Putting them into her mouth, she sucked out the moisture. Mimmīte suddenly thought of an errand for us all, and we left. On the way back to our apartment, she told us that this kind of unhygienic behavior was unacceptable.

A somewhat similar incident happened in the family of a friend of mine. We were outside playing, when her mother called her in for lunch, and my friend asked me to come along and wait. I sat there on the side as I was not invited to partake. The food smelled heavenly, and my mouth watered. They were having a milky fish soup, and a big bowl was placed in the center of the table. The family sat around it, parents, children, and grandmother. There were no individual dishes, and everyone just dipped their spoons into the liquid. Any fish-grate that came up was sucked clean and returned to the bowl. Well, I had been hungry, but now I was glad to have been left out.

A DP FAMILY LIVING IN ONE OF the smaller houses on Finkstrasse obtained a permit from the IRO to open a store in their basement to sell non-rationed produce and other merchandise. Meat was rationed so it could not be included in their wares. As a matter of fact, the Americans kept a sharp eye out for dealers of forbidden products. Otherwise, fruit and vegetables were in good supply and could be bartered from the local German farmers. The availability of new goods was conveyed by word of mouth, and the small business thrived.

Even in a DP camp as well provided as the U.S.-managed Haustetten camp, there were instances of black marketing. We never really needed additional food, but the Lithuanians were very clever. Somehow they managed to obtain a steer on the black market from a German farmer. The Americans heard about it and considered it their duty to find and confiscate the animal. They searched everywhere in the Lithuanian section without luck and finally left in exasperation. Later, one young American soldier came back alone and pleaded with the Lithuanians,

"I know you have it. I don't know where, but just out of curiosity, where is it?"

When he promised to not give them away, the Lithuanians took the man up to the attic of their block house. There they somewhat proudly showed him the forbidden steer. It was the only hiding place the Lithuanians could think of. They had had to lead the animal up the staircase, pushing and pulling the beast up to the very top. The American listened to the story in wide-eyed amazement and left shaking his head in wonder. He would never have guessed that hiding place. Well, you can lead a steer up the stairs but not down, and the Lithuanians ended up having to slaughter and butcher the animal right there in that attic.

OUR PARENTS NEVER COMPLAINED about their hardships, and that is probably how they spared us from the knowledge of the horrors of war. We never did not get the whole story, and it was necessary to catch up on a lot of what had happened from history books, and much later on the internet. There is no doubt that they and others in our refugee group had witnessed at least some of the atrocities of the war. However, our flight and the concerns for our own family made them see that everyone was in a similar boat, trying to find a peaceful and safe corner in this world. Both Maruta and I had blessedly been spared from the knowledge, understanding, and remembrance of the experiences that the grownups on our flight had to live through. The innocence of my young age along with the sheltering presence that my parents provided saw to it, and with the exception of one tragic family event, both Maruta and I were assured of a happy and normal childhood.

Unlike my cousins and a number of friends and classmates, some who had lost one parent or even both due to the circumstances of the war and the flight from Latvia, Maruta and I had both doting parents, nearby grandparents, aunts and cousins. We were a close family, and the six years spent in the limbo between our flight and our departure for the United States were for us mostly happy. Our lives were full of discoveries and experiences, and we always had friends to play with.

Still, some memories flood back from that carefree time which I could classify as not so pleasant. One such time was when a gang of children cornered a cat. When one of them said that cats always land on their feet, they decided on a demonstration. Taking the cat to the second story attic of a house, they let it fly from a window, and though they insisted that it was impossible to hurt it, I could visibly see that the animal was in pain as it hobbled away. At that age I believed almost anything that I was told, but this lie was not one of them.

Other things I just accepted. Some pearls of wisdom were imparted to me by a child no older than myself and probably just as perplexed, perhaps five years old at the time. However, her voice had the ring of authority and the knowledge of an adult, as she spoke.

"Blood is coming from her bottom and she is only nine years old."

I did not question, just listened silently in wonder, not understanding any of my friend's superior knowledge.

The stone houses in Haunstetten's DP camp surrounded an inner court of gardens, chicken coops, and the like, and we experienced life almost as if in the country. Maruta and I had our own chickens, one for each, and some families had their own garden plots, while others shared. Some grew sunflowers, and a wonderful treat was a handful of the seeds to be enjoyed. The luckiest children could be seen sitting on a bench, holding the stem of a giant sunflower head, picking the luscious seeds, and nibbling them one by one.

We also watched in grisly awe from behind bushes as a chicken was killed and readied for supper. The man had cut its neck with an axe, and the poor beast's head hung down by a thread of skin. Still, it stood and wobbled along, trailing a river of blood behind it before it finally collapsed. Some scenes we observed were just part of what we learned that life sometimes was. They were among those that were not among the gentle niceties.

One day a huge pig was brought into the camp. There in the courtyard, some five men managed to wrestle it – squealing and kicking – onto its back, trying to ready it for slaughter. A group of children had already gathered, and I too would have guiltily watched the spectacle. However, Mimmīte appeared and insisted that Maruta and I join her in a long walk away from the DP camp. We walked up a slope, but even there the distance failed to drown out the sound of the pig's squealing. Mimmīte tried to talk above the din, but it was only the pig that we heard.

Maruta recalled: "Much later, when we returned, there was the body, huge and pale, interspersed with bright red at the entrance to camp, and much later, *karbonāde,* and a blood pudding with barley."

WE HAD A THEATRE IN HAUNSTETTEN, an old wooden building near the ruins of the old Messerschmitt factory. It had an auditorium complete with a stage and a wooden plank dance floor. Looking out of the kitchen window at the night sky one autumn evening in 1947, I saw a fog of smoke and flames whipping back and forth in the distance. The theatre was on fire. For us children it was quite exciting, but not for the grownups. This had been the social hall where we had enjoyed festivals, plays, Christmas celebrations, and other happy community events, and its loss was deeply felt.

ANNIŅA AND RITA AND THEIR children were also DPs in Haunstetten. It was nice being so close to our aunts and our cousins, Valdis, Stariņ, and Daucis. Anniņa was my favorite aunt. She was my godmother and was very fond of me too. Her son Valdis was another story. Among his possessions at his home, he had children's coloring books which included connect-the-numbered-dots to make a picture. He was not a good host, and when we visited, he refused to let us use his book, but Anniņa convinced him to be a bit more generous. Grudgingly he complied, though he made us use a ruler to draw each line connecting the dots. This made it no fun at all, and I soon tired of his selfish game.

Maruta had more interactions with Valdis than I did:

> He was the camp bully. Although he and I were close and had many misadventures, there would be times when he had it in for me. In grade school, Valdis quickly gathered a group of boys around him and went looking for mischief. He'd organize a hunt, and after school, he and his gang would take off after me. I'd get home by running to the nearest two-story barracks building, dash up to the attic, and make my way to the end of the building, then run to the next one, and repeat this until I was home. From the attic dormers, I could see where he was, usually deploying his troops with "go there" arm gestures.
>
> ***
>
> Valdis and I were good at marbles. The winners would come away with the losers' marbles. Very soon, our mesh bags were bulging, and no one would risk playing with us anymore. What to do? Cross the fields to the next little village yonder? We did, and were able to leave the town heavily laden. As we were about in the middle of the field, we heard a man running at the edge, screaming at us in German. We knew from his agitated state that we certainly were not welcome there. We skedaddled back to the DP camp. Coming over the hill, we saw people running hither and yon. When we came close enough, they swarmed over us, grateful to have found the lost little dears alive. It

turned out that the field was a mined landing strip, still not cleared.

***

Once in a while, a cigarette would come our way. This was valuable, and because much coveted by the elders, valuable contraband. They'd probably not let us smoke. So up to the attic of Annie's place Valdis and I climbed and lit up. It was nasty stuff, not at all worthy of adult dedication. Somehow, we were careless with the matches, and the attic caught on fire. Frightening, but we could cope. We beat out the small fires and never did this again.

***

During one Christmas at the camp, we children were assembled in a hall to wait for Santa. He made his appearance, lugging a huge sack.

"Here are presents for all of you who have been good." He peered around.

"But there is one who has not been good this year; that one might not get a present."

I know we all inventoried our behavior, and you and I, I could tell, checking the past year, knew that we had not been all that bad.

"I have been bad," Valdis' despairing voice emerged from the assembly. "But I promise not to be that way any more."

Rita's sons Stariņ and Daucis were much nicer. However, Daucis was often mean to me, and finally I went to Rita and tattled. She soon tired of my whining.

"All right, get me a switch and I will punish Daucis," she said. Finally he will get his just reward, I thought, and running outside, broke off a branch and brought it to Rita. Disappointment followed when she gave me a hug and said,

"Daucis is my little boy, and I cannot punish him." Life was just not fair, I thought. Had I really been so vindictive at such a young age?

Stariņ was different. Maruta said, "Stariņ was a gentle boy, and when I asked him, he always pushed me in a swing, patiently and tirelessly."

THE GERMAN MONETARY unit, the *Reichsmark*, which was used from 1924, during the German Reich and the Nazi era, had already been deemed worthless in 1943. On June 20, 1948, it was officially replaced by the *Deutsche Mark* in West Germany and by the *Ostmark* in East Germany. On that day, Tētiņ went to the Landeszentralbank in Augsburg and traded in what he had left of the *Reichsmark* (RM). Each person was allowed to exchange up to 1000 RM worth of the old bills. For 817 RM that day, Tētiņ received 160 *Deutsche Mark*, still better than the official course of 10 RM for 1 DM.

IT WAS IN HAUNSTETTEN THAT Mimmīte carried out her plans for the parachute that Tētiņ had obtained while working as a locomotive stoker in Lovosice. The chute was silk and consisted of many ribbons sewn together. Mimmīte unraveled the connecting threads, dyed the strips in different colors, ironed them, and took them to the Latvian store in the basement of the house on Finkstrasse to sell as hair ribbons. Little girls at that time always wore bows in their hair, whether on top of the head or tied around the braids, as Maruta and I did. Mimmīte's ribbons were a very popular store item. Soon all little girls had the strips of brightly colored fine silk adorning their hair.

Mimmīte had always had a fondness for music, literature, and art. While living in Jelgava, she often rode her bicycle to the Opera in Rīga, a distance of 43 km., to enjoy the concerts and operas. It was her wish for her elder daughter to learn to play the violin. Mimmīte's hair ribbon project proved to be a fairly lucrative undertaking, and she earned quite a bit of money which she carefully saved. Then on October 21, 1948, she took the half-hour tram ride to Augsburg and paid a visit to the Hans Graf music store. She had had her eye on a Mittenwald Klotz violin there, and on that day she gave the store owner a partial payment of 250 DM for it. Within nine days and in two more installments, she managed to pay off the rest of the total cost of 650 DM. Now Maruta had a very fine violin. Mimmīte arranged for the violinist, Imants Gleške, who also lived in Haunstetten, to be her daughter's instructor. The whole Gleške family was very musical and eventually became professional musicians in America. Lilija Gleške was a singer, and her daughter, Laimdota, followed in her mother's footsteps.

Perhaps Mimmīte realized that the Klotz was a bit extravagant for a very young violinist, or perhaps Imants Gleške convinced her that Maruta needed a practice violin, one which would not be as great a shame if it were dropped or otherwise mistreated. So three months later, Mimmīte purchased another instrument, a Dietl for 185 DM, and probably a better candidate for the young girl to use as a practice violin. Maruta learned very quickly and well, and when we immigrated to the U.S. and Winston-Salem, North

Carolina, she became concert-master of our Wiley School's student orchestra.

THE ABILITY OF LATVIANS to come together and organize for the benefit of all was a characteristic in every DP camp in Germany. Kindergartens were one of the first things established. The smallest refugees needed something to do, friends to play with, and adult figures of authority. After kindergartens, schools were also established, and children learned with enthusiasm.

Zelma Lapsiņa, who served as the Haunstetten Girl Scout leader, became the school principal. Supplies were minimal, and much had to be improvised. When textbooks were available, they were invariably printed on newspaper stock with soft covers. These had to be shared and sometimes even copied page by page by some students, as there never were enough of them. Paper itself was in short supply. To stretch its use, the writing on Tētiņ's letters was painstakingly small, and his beautifully calligraphic script filled the paper from top to bottom and side to side.

Latvians had always exhibited a love for music. At intervals which in the beginning were a bit irregular, the people came together to establish national song festivals, the *Dziesmu Svētki*, the first of which had its start in Latvia in 1873. At that song festival a song was introduced which became Latvia's national anthem, "*Dievs, Svētī Latviju.*"

The normal scheduling of the song festival was interrupted during the Second World War. However, the festivals continued to take place in the DP camps. Latvian culture is abundant in songs handed down throughout generations. At any gathering, Latvians lift their voices in harmony. The lyrics are known to everyone, as the songs have been alive in all regions of our homeland. So it was also in the DP camps in Germany. The first song festivals in exile took place in Fischbach and Hanau in August 1946, with 16 choirs and 700 singers participating.

Spiritual lives of the DPs were also maintained during exile. An altar always found a place in the community hall of many DP camps. Many other congregations were able to hold their services in local churches. The Lutherans of the Haunstetten DP Camp were welcomed to worship in the St. Anne's church in Augsburg. Here the minister Ķullītis officiated. The first Archbishop of Latvia, Grīnbergs, paid visits to the camps. For the Christmas celebration of 1946, the Archbishop of Canterbury in England donated $1500 for the printing of song books in Latvian, providing the DP camps with 15,000 copies of the books for their church services.

MARUTA AND I WERE SOMETIMES in the same grade at school perhaps because she had been sick for quite some time and missed so much of school. We were taught religious studies, mathematics, and reading and writing Latvian. We both sang lustily in our class choir. According to our report cards, Maruta and I were better than average students with Maruta exhibiting an edge in drawing and I a bit in math. We learned cursive writing with a stylus and quill. This had to be dipped into a black inkwell, trying hard not to carry over too much of the liquid onto the paper, as it would leave a big smudge. With minor accidents, this art was also quickly mastered.

By the time we had to leave Germany, I had completed the second grade. I cannot say that I was a very good pupil, though I worked hard when I wanted to. I was very good at procrastinating, especially when there were other more fun things to do, which seemed often to be the case. Once the assignment for our class was to memorize one of the Ten Commandments. The day that we were supposed to know it, our teacher, Mrs. Šlokenberga, passed from pupil to pupil and bent an ear as she was whispered the memorized verse. I was in trouble because I had not learned it, easy though it was. Earnestly, I strained to hear it from the others as she passed from one pupil to the next. Leaning sideways, I could have fallen out of my chair as I tried to overhear the elusive murmur, but all I could make out was "bs bs bs bs." Finally she arrived at my desk. In panic, all I could do was shamelessly whisper "bs bs bs bs," into her ear. Needless to say, this did not go over very well at all.

Maruta recollects:

> I was backward because I had missed school due of various ailments, and Anniņa arranged for me to have a reading tutor, Mrs. Paudrup, a teacher in the Haunstetten school and a very good friend of hers. I remember sitting on her soft lap in her apartment, with tears oozing onto the pages, working on the words. Then, reading came too easily and I got too fond of it and astonished the class when asked to read aloud. This was to the dismay of Mimmīte, who had been so proud of our excellent eyesight. Now she saw a dark future and went on alert to keep me away from books because reading would create short-sightedness which could lead to blindness.

Maruta absolutely loved to read. She read everything that she could get her hands on. Mimmīte mistakenly thought that this would lead to Maruta's ruining her eyes. It soon became evident that her daughter might need glasses. Mimmīte was upset to the point of tears and blamed it all on the reading. After all, Papus was blind. I remember once when she was braiding Maruta's hair, she was so very angry that she started to pull it on purpose, yelling at her. Now, I don't know if this was really because Maruta had told me recently that there was no Santa Claus, or if it was because of the reading. Those two events are somewhat fused in my memory, and I know that Maruta was getting hell for both of them. I was more upset at witnessing her hair being pulled than knowing the truth about Santa Claus. Her suffering was not worth it.

When Mimmīte was in a better mood, she amused us with stories from Latvian folklore, such as those about the *Malenieki,* Latvians who live near the borders of Russia and are therefore supposedly not very bright. One story was about two *Malenieki* who go up the mountain to fell trees to build a cabin at its base. When the trees are cut, the *Malenieki* pick up one log after another, carefully carrying each one downhill. As the last one is lifted by the exhausted pair, the log slips and rolls to the clearing below.

"How stupid we are!" one exclaims. "We could have done that at the start."

With that, they pick up the logs, carry them back up, drop them, and excitedly watch them as they roll down to the bottom of the hill. This time they had done it correctly!

Another story is about the *Malenieki* building their cabin. They did not know what windows were for. So they proposed running around the meadow waving bags in the air to trap light in them. This took all day with very little results. They stopped at night because they didn't want to dilute the light that they'd already poured into the room. Such stories made us both squirm with laughter.

THEN ONE DAY IN THE FALL of 1949, I saw a great commotion with cars passing by, scouts at attention along the road, and the camp inhabitants standing, looking on, and waving in excitement.

"Who is it, what is happening?" I asked a boy who was hurrying by.

"General Eisenhower!" he called out breathlessly.

I carried this notion with me for years afterward and recounted having seen the General, who soon became the President of the United States. Much later I was corrected and it was made clear to me that it was not Eisenhower, but the Latvian ambassador to Great Britain, Kārlis Zariņš, visiting the Haunstetten DP Camp. Great Britain, the United States, and most Western powers had declined to acknowledge the seizure of the Baltics by the Soviets and even recognized the uninterrupted functioning of these countries in exile. The Ambassador had come to convey the good wishes of the people of Great Britain.

AS EARLY AS DECEMBER, 1945, President Truman issued a directive permitting the entrance of 42,000 DPs into the United States.

The news in the DP camps revolved around quota numbers. Refugees all hoped that they could somehow fit into the limitations which were being made known for each country. At the moment, almost everyone wanted to be registered for immigration to the United States. In the event that their first choices would not be realized, it was of the utmost importance to just be able to leave Germany, as living conditions there seemed to get worse by the day.

In 1948, the Displaced Persons Act, which was primarily inspired by anti-Communism, authorized the admission of 205,000 DPs over a period of two years within established though loosened quotas. If normal immigration requirements had been in place, only about 2500 people from Latvia, Estonia, and Lithuania would have been able to enter the U.S. during the course of the Act. Thus Congress had to override the restrictions, enabling the issuing of visas to Latvians to be, so to say, "mortgaged forward" to over three centuries. Under the DP Act, among the refugees admitted to the U.S., 9.3% were from Latvia, the largest number after Poland and Germany. Preference was initially given to relatives of U.S. citizens.

The majority of U.S. sponsors for DPs were churches. They could guarantee a workplace and a home directly upon the refugee's arrival in the country. It also meant that families could travel and immigrate together, and not that the father would need to go alone first to establish a home and a livelihood. However, simply registering and receiving an affidavit was no promise of acceptance for immigration. All immigrants to the U.S.A. had to undergo background and health screenings and were required to receive consular approval.

The long and extremely slow road to the fulfillment of the DP Act led to skepticism and doubt for many whether immigration to the United States would at all become a reality in the near future. Many thought it wiser to turn their attention to other countries such as Australia and Canada, as they erroneously believed that the refugees residing in the American zone would be allowed into the U.S. first. At any rate, staying in Germany posed no good prospect. The activities of the IRO would soon expire, and the Germans did not seem to have any generous inclinations toward the refugees. West Germany was already overcrowded, and every day still saw new arrivals.

Preference was finally given to those refugees who had since January 1, 1948, already resided in DP camps in American, Austrian, British, and French zones. The only requirement was that they have learned an occupation or trade, or that they possess knowledge necessary to the area to which the refugee would immigrate without robbing a citizen by replacing him in his job. The sponsor was also required to provide an assurance that the immigrant would have access to a sufficiently decent and sanitary place to live. In addition, services also would be needed to provide for the immigrant's adjustment to the new homeland. These preparations were carried out while the refugees were still overseas. Existing requirements of health and literacy were still in effect, and they were even more stringent than they had been for immigrants who were entering the country through normal channels.

Immigrants could be accompanied by their spouses and single children under the age of 21. Special allowances would be made for families headed by widowed parents.

The life of the Act would start June 30, 1948, and end on June 30, 1950. Already in the fall of 1948, the first DP families left on their way to America. Those remaining in Germany at the end after most of the refugees had departed were some 12,000 Latvians.

THROUGHOUT THE RESETTLEMENT process, the Soviets complained to their fellow Allies that the countries granting the refugees sanctuary and livelihoods were enticing them against their wishes and natural instincts to return to their own homeland. Unsatisfied with what they saw as feeble Allied efforts to return what the Soviets considered their citizens, they decided to take charge of the situation themselves. In March, 1948, *"Sovetskaja Latvija"* ("Soviet Latvia") officials visited the Austrian DP camps to try to obtain information from them about their refugees and to "invite" them to return to Latvia. In Sweden, Bolshevik agents even visited Estonian lumber workers who had already been granted asylum there.

We were continually reminded that we were justified in our intense fear and mistrust of the Soviets. We knew what often happened to people who fell prey to the Soviet wiles. The adult daughter of a Latvian refugee family in Czechoslovakia was searching for news of them when she was approached by Soviet officials. They were able to convince her that her parents and siblings had returned to Latvia, and so she decided to return also. Once there, after a lengthy and fruitless search, she realized that she had fallen into a trap from which there was no longer any escape. The young woman pleaded, "Tell every one of the Latvians in Germany to not return to Latvia. If I had known what awaited me, I would never have come back!"

NOW AND AGAIN OTHER NEWS trickled in about the current circumstances in Latvia. It was sad, even heartbreaking, to hear what was happening to our dear homeland and the people we had abandoned there.

The Soviets did their best to show the world how welcome and how successful their program was for the country. There were parades in which Latvians had to march holding placards picturing Stalin and Lenin. Upon threat of terrorism, they were forced to demonstrate their happiness at having become a part of the Soviet Union. Nevertheless, the photographs which reached the refugees in Germany showed the young women and students marching with downcast and tragic faces.

A German doctor who had been imprisoned with Latvian legionnaire POWs told of the return of prisoners from Smolensk and Kiev at the end of January 1946. At first, they had been detained together with the German POWs. Later, when the vehicles transported them from the station to Meža Park in Rīga, a number of the legionnaires fell out of the transport already dead. Others, unable to walk, had to be carried or otherwise supported. They were then confined in separate camps from which some were later freed. Although the doctor later observed them in civilian dress, he soon heard that they all had been sentenced to ten to fifteen years of forced labor.

20,000 Latvian civilians were detained in a concentration camp in Rīga. The inmates, ranging in age from twelve to seventy, were forced to work but received little nourishment. Every day many died for lack of food or medicine. Later, the camp was moved to Meža Park, not far from the German

POW camp, and a wooden fence three meters high surrounded it.

During his Latvian sojourn, the German doctor spoke with three voluntarily repatriated refugees, all of whom deeply regretted returning to Latvia. The doctor was convinced that the goal of the Soviets was to annihilate the Latvian nation, step by step.

DURING THE FIRST POST-WAR YEARS in Latvia, the Soviets were eager to have their burden eased. This meant deportation or imprisonment, in Gulags or concentration camps, of citizens who could possibly pose a threat or were even a minor obstacle to their planned program for Soviet Latvia. A few lucky individuals managed to avoid or escape arrest, and many of these joined the Forest Brothers.

In the Cold War era, mass deportations were again conducted from the three Baltic States. Code named Operation Priboi, some 90,000 people were sent to Siberia and other unlivable places within Russia. The removal of those deemed "enemies of the people" attained its highest point in March 1949. This was supposed to remove any resistance to the collectivization of the Latvian farms and to drain the support for the Forest Brothers partisans. Neighbor did not confide in neighbor, and letters to other places were simply not sent. Just the receipt of mail from abroad was considered to be a ticket to Siberia.

On a regular basis, two to three times per month, eastward bound trains left Latvia to transport goods to the Russian interior and farther east. Connected to them were at least four or five wagons full of civilians. The poor unfortunates had been roused from their sleep and chased out of their homes in the city. Under strong NKVD secret police guard, they were brought to the station for the journey. Each wagon contained about fifty persons. Women were heard screaming and children crying as the guards roughly pushed them, even the infants, into the train wagons. Another shipment thus left for Siberia. On board, the Soviets claimed, were the Soviet Latvian citizens who had "volunteered." In expectation of what might become the inevitable, each Latvian kept a small packet of necessary clothing and items at the ready to quickly grab when eventually they too were compelled to take part on that very same journey.

The deportations finally served their purpose, and within a few weeks, the majority of the rural households accepted collectivization. Agriculture, the backbone of the Latvian economy in the 1930s, had finally collapsed.

The armed resistance by the Forest Brothers was also greatly hindered, first by NKVD infiltrators, then by double agents. The last Forest Brothers group finally surrendered in 1957, though one notable hold-out, Jānis Pīnups, who had deserted from the Red Army in 1944, came out of hiding only in 1995.

German POWs still in Latvia in 1949 and waiting to be repatriated to Germany told about their lives during these past years since the war's end. They had not met anyone positively inclined toward the Soviets, but had to pretend to be in order to protect their lives. Latvians hopelessly longed for the resumption of the war so that the Soviets could perhaps be driven out of their homeland.

A young woman who secretly brought food to the German POWs was imprisoned by the NKVD. Later, she was forced to spy on the Germans, to which she reluctantly had to agree. Nevertheless, after two weeks, nothing more was heard of her.

The news of legionnaires returning from Germany was also very grim. They all had been extradited to the Murmansk region of Russia. Those deemed not guilty were sentenced to one to two years hard labor. Others who had been found guilty received a sentence of fifteen to twenty-five years forced labor and were sent even farther north.

IN 1947 LATVIAN NEWSPAPERS reported that of 5700 buildings in Jelgava, 4580 had been destroyed. In Rīga, Latvians eagerly awaited renovation work for the St. Peter church tower and also the Blackheads building. Leveled buildings generally were not replaced, and the ruins remained as sad witness to Latvia's tragedy. Letters from Latvia destined for overseas had been dictated by the Cheka. To not overwhelm the recipients with too many impossible wonders, the Bolsheviks also allowed an iota of truth to be mixed in with all of the propaganda.

The elegance of the capital of Rīga had changed dramatically and was unrecognizable. The beautiful flowers along the walkways were no more, and the streets were dirty and unkempt. More Russians than Latvians populated the city. In every Latvian farm at least one Russian family had been deposited to supervise and hound the resident Latvians. Crime was a regular daily occurrence. In the coming summer, it was announced that yet another kolkhoz would soon be established.

In Rīga, people were able to receive food, though the lines at stores were terribly long. In 1948, Latvians there had no other option but to sell their valuables and clothing in order to buy nourishment and to pay for heating. If caught at this, as it was considered black marketing, they were sentenced to forced labor and exiled.

Doctors were sometimes allowed a private practice if they chose, but were taxed excessively if they did. The alternative was to remain in public service, where the salary they received was insufficient to pay for their family's needs. Other doctors were imported from areas of the new "expansive homeland" where the education they had received was markedly inferior to that of Latvian doctors.

UNDER SOVIET RULE, LATVIA BECAME completely isolated from the outside world. The flourishing social and cultural contacts which it had once shared with the West were cut off, and now its only communication was with other nations which the Soviets had absorbed.

In coming years, Soviet Russia infiltrated itself even more into what had once been Latvia. Especially because of the country's success during the years of its independence, the Soviets decided to continue that work in Latvia. To that end, they imported their own workers and specialists to take over the factories, plants, and infrastructure. With this influx, they also brought their language, and it was spread through all spheres of their lives. Russian became the compulsory language of all schools and industry. Official business was now conducted only in that language, and everyone had to master it. The Russification of Latvia was complete and the Latvian language became a minority in its own country.

Nevertheless, our native language remained alive in Latvian homes and in Latvian hearts. In 2003, during my first visit to Latvia since our family's flight in 1944, I whiled a bit at the Freedom Monument. A celebration had taken place there during which everyone sang the Latvian National Anthem. At the end, I talked a little with a gentleman, perhaps somewhat older than me. To each other we expressed our joy that events like this were taking place in Rīga.

Before we parted, he said to me, "Thank you that you are still speaking Latvian."

I answered him, "Thank you also that you are still speaking Latvian." About this, I need not have worried.

Haunstetten - I was very proud of my national costume.

Kindergarten in Haunstetten. I am in the doorway.

Haunstetten school teachers.
1st row: Brigita Valta, Gunārs Saliņš, Jautrīte Saliņa, Zelma Lapsiņa, Arvīds Lapsiņš, Eiženija Zintniece
2nd row: Briedis, ?, Lūcija Kalniņa, Ludmilla Birne, Erniņa, Tamāra Šlokenberga, Delviga, Mirdza Paudrupe, Modris Bergmanis

Maruta is walking by on the left.

A children's festival in Haunstetten

Dagnija and Maruta on the way to school.

Haunstetten DP Camp policemen:
Mr. Ēversons and Alfrēds Neimanis

Lidija and Alfrēds Neimanis

Our family. This photograph was sent to our future sponsors in America.

A sketch by Ansis Bērziņš

An intarsia by Alfrēds Neimanis
based on a sketch by Ansis Bērziņš

After Munich – balloons, Topsy, Birucītis, and the intarsia press in the lower corner in the photo on the right

Block houses of DP Camp Haunstetten on Flachsstrasse
We lived in the third and farthest one.
Homes of former Messerschmitt workers.

School and workshop buildings of the DP Camp
The forced laborers formerly occupied these buildings.

Maruta with a violin that a parachute bought.

Saying good-bye to our teacher, Mrs. Jurševska, who emigrated to Australia in October 1949

CHAPTER FIFTEEN

MAMMA AND PAPUS

I don't know for how long Mamma had already suffered from asthma, but as it got worse, probably already in the 1930s, she was being treated in the sanatorium in Tērvete, Latvia, 31 km. southwest of Jelgava. Then, after fleeing from Latvia, when we lived first in the Lauingen camp and later in the Haunstetten DP camp, Mamma remained as a patient in the sanatorium in Amberg, the first town in Germany to which we arrived after fleeing Czechoslovakia.

From the time that she was in Amberg, we heard from her mostly through her letters. The illness did not prevent her from writing, and her handwriting always seemed firm and steady. She wrote about books she read, instructed us on how to make tea from pine branch shoots, told about the various opinions of her prognoses from her doctors, and even discussed the laboratory results of her blood tests. She told about hearing from her sister Aleksandra, our "Tante Sanna." Aleksandra was a former nurse who, after the war, ended up in London and found a job in a hospital.

"She is used to her work and is pleased that, though her room is small, it is warm, and she has enough to eat." However, Tante Sanna was afraid of losing her job because her hands sometimes shook.

Some doctors told Mamma that her heart was to blame for her shortness of breath. Others told her that if she stops taking her asthma medication, her heart would improve. So Mamma stopped taking the medication. However, she noted that there was no remarkable improvement and her condition varied from day to day.

"At least I do not spend any more money on the medicine, and perhaps the thought of its expense had also aggravated my heart."

She wrote us about a Latvian minister named Kaktiņš, a bacteriologist with the title of Professor, who was "treating asthma with a vaccine derived from patients' saliva."

Sometimes she complained about the daily drudgery. "We are required to sleep very much. This is so difficult if one is not tired. The daily sleeping times are 8:30 to 11:30, 12:30 to 3:00, 3:30 to 5:30. Evenings we have to go to sleep at 9:30."

Mamma also sometimes sent us a package:

> Socks for Marutiņa, so her feet would not get cold during the night. They were knitted by a healthy acquaintance.

> That lady could also knit something for Daģītis. The yarn has been washed, and the socks were wetted and ironed with a hot iron. She is a very kind lady who helps me a lot and brings back whatever I need from town.

Another time, Mamma sent some grapes and chocolates for Stariņ and emphasized having handled the grapes only by the stem.

Her news was always about the comings and goings around herself and the things that she observed. So it was not unusual that on July 15, 1949, when she wrote what was to be her last letter to us, its content was not any more foreboding. This letter, like the others, was in her even neat handwriting, and there was no hint about the days to come. Mamma lamented that she did not have better communication with the doctors, who seemed to talk to the patients as if they were children. For that reason she was resigned to judging her own state of health and concluded that it was definitely not getting better. She longed to be able to observe her grandchildren at play. Mamma suggested that they be persuaded to go for walks with Papus. She told of her own grandfather who had offered five kopeks to his grandchildren to accompany him.

On July 20, 1949, when Hermanis went to visit Mamma in the Amberg sanatorium, he was met by the doctor, who told him that his mother is dying and will undoubtedly pass away during the night.

Hermanis could not accept the doctor's prognosis. When he protested, the doctor's reply was, "We know she will die."

So the nursing staff pushed Mamma's bed into what at the hospital was known as the "dying room." Hermanis stayed there and sat with his mother so that she would not be alone. However, after a while he dozed off, and when he awoke, Mamma had already passed away.

That same evening, Mimmīte had taken the train to visit Mamma. Getting off at the station, she had a strange premonition and felt that she needed to get to the sanatorium as quickly as possible. Out of breath, she arrived at the institution's door and found that her fear was justified when the watchman on duty informed her that Mamma had died during the night.

Anniņa recounted her own experience. The same night that Mimmīte had taken the train to visit Mamma, Anniņa came to our home in Haunstetten with Valdis. She put us all to bed, even told us a little story, and we fell asleep. Suddenly, while sitting in the stillness, an unusual feeling came over her, and she observed an illumination, an apparition of Mamma's figure standing in the doorway to our room, the same doorway at which Papus had stood, as he, Maruta, and I sang our evening song, *Nu Es Gribu Gulēt Iet* (Now I Lay Me Down to Sleep). Mamma appeared dressed as in the old days in Latvia, and the bright light surrounding her made the dress glisten. She gazed at all three children, one after the other, and then disappeared. Anniņa glanced at her watch. It showed 11:45 at night. In the morning, the telegram arrived that Mamma had died at that very hour. Anniņa said that it was very strange, and she couldn't understand it. Mamma had stood there, so lovely in the dress that she had given her a long time ago, looking at her beloved family. She said that Mamma did not die of asthma, but rather of a ruptured hernia, the result of her intense coughing.

Now and again Anniņa described her experiences with the paranormal, the voices and apparitions ranging from

Mamma to Jesus. As she had done now and again during the flight from Latvia, Anniņa often ascribed celestial intervention to mundane events. Perhaps it served to explain a lot of the confusion and mystery of life to her, and she accepted that which she perceived without question. It made life much easier to comprehend.

When it was time, Mimmīte, Rita, and Anniņa went into town and obtained a coffin for Mamma's funeral. Mrs. Braslis also attended. She was a very good friend, the woman who had made Maruta's and my first Latvian folk costumes. Otherwise, only the minister was present at the funeral. Hermanis could not be there, as he had to be back with his *Melnie* company in Stuttgart. News of the funeral was kept from Papus. Anniņa thought that he should have been told, but Rita's opinion prevailed. Later, when they were back in Haunstetten, Papus told them, "I know what you were doing."

After Mamma died, one night while Anniņa was sleeping, she heard a voice speaking to her.

"Your mother died on Wednesday, and your father will also die on Wednesday."

Anniņa had never called her parents "mother and father," so it was very odd, she said. The voice was very clear, in Latvian.

"Father also died."

Anniņa protested, "But Papus is alive! Mamma died!"

"Mother died on Wednesday. Father will also die on Wednesday." And in two months on a Wednesday, Papus died.

"I think that it was already then when Mamma died, Papus practically died with her, because with her passing, he lost everything," Anniņa explained.

I do not have any memory of Mamma other than the photos of the slight and delicate woman, and I have to rely on the stories told to me by her children and also her letters to our family to gain a bit of knowledge. Later, after Mamma's passing, as the thought of death overwhelmed me, I lay in Mimmīte's warm embrace, sobbing and telling her my fears because the thought of ghosts was terrifying. Mimmīte comforted me.

"Mamma is now your guardian angel and loves you and will always protect you," she said. This brought much comfort and assurance, and I was no longer afraid.

PAPUS LIVED WITH OUR FAMILY in Haunstetten in the kitchen which was shared by the inhabitants of the other apartment. His bed was in the corner beyond the central kitchen table, right outside the door of the room where the rest of our family slept. Beside his bed was a chair, and above that on a shelf was his radio, to which he listened constantly, as he was blind, and this was his only pastime. He had it turned on softly, and he would sit there on the chair, bending his head toward the sound, listening to news of current events. He also had some books in Braille which he read and reread, and relived the stories that the Braille paper bumps would tell, sometimes over and over, as the books he had were very few. He was gentle to us his granddaughters, swinging us on the instep of his foot upon request, and as Maruta recounted, telling us stories of what life had been like in ancient Greece.

Papus sometimes remarked, "How I wish that I could see you all!"

Anniņa said that Papus became blind gradually, starting already sometime around 1919 or so. It was due to retinal detachment, Stariņ said. It must have been a very sad time for him then.

On occasion in Haunstetten, there were former students, now also fellow DPs, from the school in Jelgava, the *Hercoga Pētera Ģimnāzija,* who came and visited. They would sit there in the kitchen and speak among themselves of the time when he had been their classics professor. There were shouted greetings, laughter, and noisy discourse as they remembered the school and the students they all had known. This was rather startling, because we were used to the daily hush which surrounded Papus. To us, Mimmite always said to be still, that Papus did not like noise, so this must have been very special.

Most evenings, Papus would come and stand in the doorway, and together, he, Maruta, and I would sing the evening prayer, *Nu Es Gribu Gulēt Iet*, as we lay in our beds. He did not come into the room, but stood there at the door, one hand resting on the door frame, looking blindly into space as we sang our song. Then when we finished, he bade us good-night and felt his way back to his own bed in the kitchen.

AS THE TIME APPROACHED for us to emigrate, all kinds of plans were being made. By now, our family had found sponsors in North Carolina, but we still had to get the OK for the immigration to take place. Presently, however, we received the incomprehensible news that the emigration for Papus had not been authorized. He was almost 80 years old, blind, and in too fragile a state of health, and the IRO denied it.

Already in August, 1949, the DP communities encountered days of despair. Without any previous explanation, IRO started to implement actions which had already been decided in Geneva the previous year. This included instances of forced repatriation or forced emigration to countries to which the refugees had no desire to travel. Sometimes IRO representatives appeared in DP camps and demanded that within 24 hours the refugees produce documental proof that they are scheduled for emigration, as everyone who qualified had been required to do. All DPs would be allocated into groups in progressively diminishing precedence. The first group was made up of those who would agree to voluntary repatriation, followed by those having a guarantee of immigration to the U.S.A. or to another preferred country, after which came those who, because of age or invalid status, would be destined to remain in the care of a charitable organization. Papus was allocated into the last group, and our family was notified that he would have to stay in Germany.

The news was a deep shock to all of us, and his daughters were at a loss for how to handle the situation. It seemed to be such an inhumane act on the part of IRO. The three sisters, Rita, Lidija, and Anniņa would take him for walks to enjoy the fresh air. On one occasion, when they sat down to talk, Anniņa spoke to him.

"Papu, I won't leave without you. I won't leave you alone anywhere!"

He turned to her and said, "Is that really what you are planning?"

Anniņa answered him, "Yes, exactly that." She had made up her mind.

Many years later, telling me about this, she explained.

"And that's exactly as it came about. When we did emigrate, just as promised, I took both of their urns with me. We had bought them for Mamma and Papus in Augsburg at the cemetery. They asked if I would bury them, and I replied, 'yes.'"

THEN CAME THE DAY, SEPTEMBER 9, 1949, when I awoke to voices and commotion and the sound of feet shuffling about. I did not know what had happened, just that something seemed terribly wrong. Maruta and I were not told anything. We just saw that Mimmīte was crying and Tētiņ could not console her, and there were other people who came and went. We were taken to another house to be looked after while our parents and aunts sorted things out. That night, Mimmīte, even more inconsolable, had us all sleep on the floor together and close, and she was still crying so much that I could not fall asleep.

At one point she screamed at Tētiņ, "You know how light he was. You helped carry him down the stairs! He didn't eat anything at all."

It finally dawned on me that Papus had died.

That day, playing outside, some kids called Maruta over and almost viciously taunted her, saying that Papus had killed himself. A few days after the funeral, she read about it in a newspaper and knew that it was true. I, however, remained in ignorance about the reason for his death until my adulthood.

It was years later that Anniņa told me that it was Mimmīte who discovered Papus, who'd hanged himself in the attic. She had seen that his bed was empty, and not knowing where he could be, she finally went up to the attic and found him there. Papus could not have it on his conscience that Anna and her son would have to stay in Germany for his sake. Anniņa had told him that she would never leave him, and the guilt that he was the cause – this he could not bear, so Papus took his life into his own hands.

In Haunstetten, a funeral took place a few days after my grandfather's death. Many mourners, all in somber attire, were gathered from both of the Augsburg DP camps and from other camps in Bavaria. Among them were other blind refugees. I stayed very close to Mimmīte, clutching her hand in my bid for comfort. At the cemetery, we saw bodies displayed behind rain-smeared glass. The coffins were tipped at an angle, as if in a showroom to enable proper viewing from the outside. I wondered about them, and Mimmīte said that they were not real people, but mannequins displayed for the bereaved to look at. My cousin, Daucis, gripping his mother's hand, cried inconsolably. Then when they all were to go in for the viewing, Maruta and I were left outside to wait.

Anniņa never did abandon her promise, and when she and Valdis finally immigrated to America, it was with the urns of the ashes of both Marta and Eduards Bištēviņš. These she eventually had buried in the Latvian section of Woodlawn Cemetery in Grand Rapids, Michigan, where she settled. Anniņa purchased two plots in the cemetery – one which would hold both of her parents' urns, and next to that another plot for herself. Even then, it had a headstone with her name on it. She also purchased two additional plots at the head of these, where she planted a linden tree like the many lindens that she loved in Latvia. She did not want the hot sun to shine on the graves, but rather for them to be sheltered by the tree's branches. Years later, when I visited Anniņa in Grand Rapids, we always went to the cemetery and placed fresh flowers on the grave. I took some leaves from the linden and pressed them to keep for a memory.

My most enduring memories of Papus remain the evenings when he came to the door of the room where we slept in Haunstetten and sang the evening prayer with us. That is my last fond remembrance of him. Maruta said, "The night he died, Papus did not come to the door to sing our song. I felt that if he had, he would not have done what he did."

PAPUS HAD BEEN A WELL-KNOWN and revered personage in the Latvian DP community, and his death and tragic story were reported on the first page of the newspaper *Latvija* on September 14, 1949, and also in other local editions. (The book, *DPs Europe's Displaced Persons, 1945-1951*, by Mark Wyman, was published the U.S. in 1989. In it is a paragraph reminiscent of Papus' story, and having read it, I contacted the author and inquired about his reference. Mark Wyman sent me the requested copy, and of course, it was about our grandfather, Eduards Bištēviņš.)

His suicide and the reason behind it caused an international outcry against what many considered to be inhumane IRO policies. Memoranda expressing the protest of the Latvian community were sent to both London and Washington. These noted that because of regulations, twenty-five to thirty thousand refugees would be doomed to remain in Germany and Austria, among them war invalids, orphans, large families, and the aged.

Already in 1947, there were more than a thousand orphans living in the DP camps in Germany. They languished without the warmth of their families or godparents. Fellow DPs were encouraged to open their hearts by sending them a bit of money or a small package to help fill the void caused by the tragic parental absences. Some countries were already accepting orphans, but it was not until 1949 that the U.S., sponsored by the Lutheran World Federation, would do so. Our parents had always assured us that in case anything would ever happen to them, our godparents were there to look after us and love us. This was a relief and another reminder that we need not worry about our welfare.

Because of the problems coming to light in the selection process, actions were initiated to help solve those of refugees who would otherwise have been doomed to uncertain futures. One Ukrainian couple was initially rejected for emigration because the wife had an eye ailment. Another couple was turned down because the wife was illiterate. In the latter case, the couple's emigration to Australia was finally allowed when the husband promised to teach his wife to read during the voyage.

Perhaps motivated by the reason of our grandfather's suicide, Norwegians urged their country to allow the immigration of a hundred blind DP refugees. Other countries finally agreed to accept people with TB, invalids, aged persons, and those thought to be overlooked for selection—the scientists, artists, and others with unordinary livelihoods.

In the latter case, the Pakistani General Faruki, himself a doctor by profession, endeavored to help his colleagues. He learned that doctors who immigrate to the U.S.A. would not be able to practice their learned profession but were resigned to working as waiters and manual laborers. Some two thousand of them were still without an assured future. General Faruki proposed that fifty of these physicians be designated for immigration to Pakistan, and there to be allowed to practice their profession without having to be reeducated for the purpose of obtaining the required certificates. In this he succeeded, and thus Pakistan became the first country to accept DP doctors, several of whom were Latvians.

IN THE MIDST OF THIS GOOD NEWS, efforts were still ongoing to repatriate refugees to their own countries. The Soviet Union claimed that Estonians, Lithuanians, and Latvians were Soviet citizens, and Soviet liaison officers were thereby allowed to visit DP centers to try to persuade the Baltic refugees to return to their native countries. Only about 1% repatriated and many of these were ex-prisoners of war who longed to rejoin their families which remained in their native countries. Since the start of the Soviet occupation of Latvia, orphanages had been established in Rīga for the children of absent legionnaires. No doubt a number who returned were the fathers of these orphans.

Despite IROs efforts, which included reducing the caloric daily allowance to 1550 per day, the majority of Latvians resisted deportation. They would rather starve than find themselves in Soviet hands. The international community soon realized that repatriation efforts to Latvia would not work.

SOON OTHER COUNTRIES STARTED selectively accepting refugees. Single women and widows were urged to seek refuge in Australia. Single men had the easiest time to emigrate, as they were the most sought by countries needing workers for repairing war-demolished infrastructures. Belgium was the first country to offer jobs to some 20,000 DPs, as it needed cheap labor in the coal mines. At times, refugees had to accept immigration to countries to which they did not wish to go. Still, even this was preferable to staying in Germany.

Though the U.S.A. was one of the last countries to open its gates, it did so to the largest number, accepting some 400,000 refugees within its borders. The necessity of being matched to affidavits was very worrisome. These were guarantees stating that refugees would not pose a problem to those Americans already employed by having them lose their jobs in favor of the new arrivals, or that they would become a burden on society. Many refugees would be sponsored by churches which already guaranteed an employment and a place to live. However, they were a minority. Other refugees had to accept any kind of job which they would be offered, in some cases even those considered to be demeaning. To hasten their departure, refugees insisted that they would gladly accept any job offered to them.

As the last of the DPs left, the empty camps were shut down one by one, and the homes taken from the Germans finally reverted back to their owners. By 1952, only one camp for refugees still remained in operation.

At the closing of the refugee DP camps, others were established. These were for the ill and the aged: those not able or not allowed to emigrate, or incapable of starting independent lives outside the camp. Perhaps this is where IRO had intended for Papus to spend the last years of his life.

THE LUTHERAN WORLD FEDERATION was charged with matching prospective sponsors in America to DPs in Germany. Our family had the good fortune to have the Augsburg Lutheran Church guarantee sponsorship. This was in Winston-Salem, North Carolina, and so the preparations for emigration began. Soon we were in correspondence with our American benefactor and chief usher of the church, G. W. Barkley. Even Maruta and I were encouraged to send letters and pictures of ourselves to Mr. Barkley's daughters, Lucille and Marie.

In the school in Haunstetten, we had some instruction in English, at least enough of it to write the awkward letters to the Barkley girls. After moving to Hochfeld upon the closing of the Haunstetten DP camp, we did not have school any more. At that time teachers themselves were already emigrating, and at any rate, there was just too much going on.

We were pleased to be going to Winston-Salem, since the Platais family, including Mammucītis, were already in the somewhat nearby Shelby, North Carolina. They had already immigrated in October of 1949. Jānis Platais' sister, Ina Meisters' family arrived later in June 1950 and also settled in North Carolina. So it seemed almost inevitable, following the period of time that it took our parents to work off their debt to the Augsburg Lutheran Church for the sponsorship which we received, that the whole extended Neimanis – Platais family eventually ended up together in the Milwaukee area.

AMONG THE PREPARATIONS necessary for the closing of the Haunstetten DP camp and our move to the nearby Hochfeld camp was to find a new home for our two chickens. Neither Mimmīte nor Tētiņ were insensitive to Maruta's and my feelings about the dear little beasts. No, we would not have them for supper, but Mimmīte talked us into allowing her to give them to a nice German lady who lived nearby. The chickens would have friends there, she said, as the lady already had a chicken coop and also a daughter who would love to take care of them. Sadly, we agreed. Our benefactress was very grateful, and as thanks, invited Maruta and me to come for a visit and spend an afternoon with her daughter.

We did not understand each other, but they were really very nice people, and whenever the lady addressed us, she did so smiling kindly. I remember looking over all of their chickens, trying to find our two pets, to no avail. I hoped desperately that they were off somewhere just having fun, but I think that it was wishful thinking. I asked Maruta if she saw them, but she had to tell me that she did not. I suspected the worst, but did not have the courage to voice my opinion. If I did not say anything, the thought would go away. I don't remember what they served us, but I hoped that it was not chicken. After lunch we helped the daughter of the house wash the dishes. How curious, they used soap in their dishwater.

Our preparations for emigration started slowly. We all had to be vaccinated against smallpox, and this was already carried out in April 1949. Smallpox at the time was still a concern, and all refugees had to at one time or another be immunized. We were aware that the scratches on the skin would give us two initial round pox, which, when healed, would become huge round scars. Mimmīte, always considerate of the appearance of her two girls, insisted that the vaccines be done on the leg. All the other children had them on the upper arm, and these round circles were always visible when wearing a sleeveless outfit. I was grateful to Mimmīte for her foresight, but growing up, I still tried to cover my upper left leg when in a bathing suit. After all, Maruta had her two round scars horizontally near her swimsuit line, but mine were spaced one above the other, sometimes reaching below the hem of the shorts I wore.

SHORTLY BEFORE THE EMIGRATION from Germany, we had a family get-together at which a collection of the Bištēviņš family is visible on the family photographs. There I am with Topsy in my arms. I had been ill with fever shortly before this gathering and still looked a bit tousled. Anniņa was there with her son Valdis, Rita with Daucis and Stariņ, Hermanis, and Alīse and her husband Pulkvedis Silenieks. It was the last time that we all as a family gathered together. Judging from the pictures, it was close to Christmas. An Advent wreath with candles is hanging from the ceiling. We all were there to say good-by to Rita's family, who emigrated in December 1949, sailing on the *USAT General Muir,* and arriving in New York two days after Christmas. After them,

Alīse and her husband departed for America, finally settling in Des Moines, Iowa, and living out their lives in close proximity to the Kalniņš family. Anniņa and her son Valdis, along with the ashes of our grandparents, were the last to sail – in July 1950. I think that we and our relatives were close, judging from the collection of various family photographs, and I often regret the separation that the war forced upon us all.

Alīse was the daughter of Papus' sister, "Lisetti." Alīse's brother, Artūrs Uice, his wife, and son Ilmārs did not emigrate, but remained in their home, Velves, near Jelgava. After the war in Europe, the family was evicted by the Soviets. In their place, they planted a collection of Russians who commenced to treat the beloved home like pigs. Later, Ilmārs managed to build a house for his family in Jelgava, doing so with his own two hands. Now and then Mimmīte received letters from her cousin Ilmārs, and more recently after the rebirth of Latvia's independence, I have visited with Ilmars' son Ēriks and his family.

Papus' brother Indriķis, the landlord of Bākuļi (the birthplace of Papus and his siblings) and his wife Olga stayed, but their sons emigrated. Indriķis' older son, Valdis Bištēviņš and his family, settled in Ventura, California. Olģerts Bištēviņš, Indriķis' younger son, the orchestra conductor, took his family first to Sweden and then made a permanent home in Argentina. And so we are now all scattered to the far reaches of the earth. Bākuļi did not fare any better than Velves, as the old Bištēviņš couple was evicted to make way for more Soviet infiltrators. Though the Uice family was able to reposses Velves long after Latvia's 1991 rebirth, Bākuļi is still inhabited by residents who screech like monkeys at the sight of any visitors. I suspect that they would burn the house down rather than surrender it.

As DPs started emigrating, some camps needed to be consolidated. Our Haunstetten camp was still active, and the school stayed open until January 4, 1950, shortly before we had to move to the Hochfeld camp.

WHEN IT BECAME KNOWN THAT those who had left for the U.S.A. did not fare very well in the crossing due to seasickness, it was announced to the refugees that IRO would supply future departees with *Dramamine*. In case of storms on the Atlantic, they were instructed to take the tablets three times per day. Some emigrees complained that even this did not help.

Mamma in the Amberg sanatorium,
above, left, with Hermanis.

Below, Mamma is seated on the right with fellow patients,
probably during Easter festivities.

Mamma's funeral in Amberg.

Pictured are Lidija, Rita, Mrs. Braslis, Anniņa

Papus

Papus and Mimmīte are at the entrance to Flachsstrasse 60, having returned from getting a pail of milk.

Farewell get-together. Standing on left: Alfrēds and Lidija.
Others: P. Silenieks, Valdis, Alīse, Maruta, Dagnija, Rita, Stariņ, Daucis.

December, 1949. The first to emigrate, Rita and her sons.

CHAPTER SIXTEEN

HOCHFELD, January 1950, AND GRONAU

In early 1950, Haunstetten was shut down as a DP center, and on January 11, our family was temporarily moved to Hochfeld, another DP camp in the Augsburg area just some six km. from Haunstetten, where Tētiņ worked as a watchman.

While in Hochfeld, we learned that items of value obtained in Germany could not be exported. This was worrying and confusing for everyone, as only a handful of refugees had not obtained something valuable during their five to six year stay in Germany. In order to be able to take along the two previously acquired violins and also the Rolleiflex camera which we had recently bartered from

Hermanis, fellow DPs made "Depositions of Witnesses" for each other, stating that they were aware that the items in our possession had been transported from Latvia and were therefore exportable. These were necessary white lies which saved our possessions, and nobody could possibly be hurt by them.

For transporting the bulk of their belongings to the U.S.A., all DP families were required to have a crate constructed of wood to specifications of uniform measurements which turned out to be less than a third of a cubic meter. These would be carried in the hold of the ship. Articles necessary for the ship's voyage itself had to be packed into a suitcase for the passengers. Female and male passengers were to have different suitcases, as the communal sleeping quarters for the two sexes would be separate.

That massive iron press which an ironmonger had fashioned for Tētiņ in Augsburg probably was not considered of as much value as to be included in the depositions by the witnesses, but its weight, nonetheless, posed a slight problem. Though no weight limit was ascribed to the wooden crates, after hauling those of other DPs, the Americans wanted to know why Tētiņ's was so much heavier, and they demanded that he open it for inspection. They had to be sure that he was not transporting weapons of any kind. Besides the press, a collection of wood veneers were also taken along.

On April 26, 1950, in Hochfeld, we were declassified from the DP rolls and stricken from the residency lists. With white numbered tags pinned to our lapels, we travelled by train from Hochfeld to Gronau, the transitional DP camp in the British zone near Bremerhafen. There we waited for about a week to be assigned to a ship which would take us to America.

THE DISPLACED PERSONS COMMISSION located in Washington, DC, provided informational leaflets to all refugees destined for the U.S.A. One, written in German, explained the duties of all Displaced Persons to repay their benefactors the cost of their transport to the United States. This expense, and that of a place of residence were to be repaid by the refugees through employment, during which time they would receive subsistence wages. In this way sponsors gained help for their farms, or in Tētiņ's case, the Augsburg Lutheran Church in Winston-Salem acquired a caretaker. The other informational note was in English, requiring the new immigrants to report twice a year for two years on their progress of life in the United States.

Tētiņ said that Mimmīte became depressed at the thought of leaving, since she had a foreboding that she would never again be able to return. When it came time to leave, Mimmīte feigned illness, hoping to be allowed to stay, but this came to naught. There was no other way about it. We all had to emigrate.

For the young people, going to America was a new adventure. The resilience of their young minds and bodies made that easy. Those who were older boarded the ships with feelings somewhere between hope and apprehension. They had spent six years in exile fraught with dangers, and now experienced the relief of knowing that their endeavors had all been worthwhile.

Still, in their minds they were Latvians, and their children were Latvians. Many of them had only one thought in common: to return to Latvia and take up our interrupted lives once more. Even while we lived comfortably in America, Latvians at every get-together reminisced about their homeland. There was unity in the desire and their goal to once more return. This was not to be ungrateful to America for her very generous actions on behalf of us refugees. It was simply what the heart yearns for.

TĒTIŅ SAVED A LITTLE SHEET of hymns that were sung during the last church service we attended in Hochfeld. It was held on April 23, 1950, and Provost Ķullītis and the Reverend Upīte officiated. In the last stanza of the last hymn, to the melody of *Jēzus dzīvo mūžīgi*, we sang the words,

Lai tad ceļš pa miglu iet,
Lai kā viļņos mētāts tieku,
Tak pie Tevis turos ciet',
Cerību uz Tevi lieku.
Tu caur as'ru ieleju
Vedīsi uz svētību.

Though our path leads through the fog,
Though through turbulent waves we are tossed,
I know that I am in Your care,
My faith is in You.
Through the valley of tears
To grace You will lead us.

ON MAY 4, 1950, five years, six months, and twenty-seven days after fleeing Latvia, with new *C.C. Ballou* identification tags pinned to our chests, our family boarded the American troop transport ship *General C.C. Ballou* and set sail from Bremerhafen to our new life in the United States of America. Tētiņ noted that the time of our departure was 3:30 in the afternoon.

Saying farewell to friends and family in Bremerhafen shortly before boarding the *General C.C. Ballou*

Photo courtesy of Valters Nollendorfs

The troop carrier, the *General C.C. Ballou* in Bremerhafen on May 4, 1950, with passengers waiting to board.

AFTERWORD

In the summer of 2003, Maruta, my daughter Rachel, and I returned to Džūkste to bury our parents' ashes. As we stood at the grave, we could look beyond the ruins of the church and see the old post office building. I think that both Tētiņ and Mimmīte would have approved.